MW01596763

Expert Witnessing
in Forensic
Accounting

Walter J. Pagano
Thomas A. Buckhoff
Editors

Edwards

ISBN: 1-930217-14-5
ISSN 1524-5586

Edwards   www.rtedwards.com

Library of Congress Cataloging-in-Publication Data

Expert witnessing in forensic accounting / Walter J. Pagano, Thomas Buckhoff, editors.
    p. cm.
"ISSN 1524-5586."
Includes bibliographical references and index.
ISBN 1-930217-14-5 (alk. paper)
1. Forensic accounting--United States. 2. Evidence, Expert--United States. I. Pagano, Walter J., 1951- II. Buckhoff, Thomas A.
KF8968.15.E97 2005
347.73'67--dc22
                        2005011510

    1 2 3 4 5 LS 5 6 7 8 9
Printed in the United States of America

CONTENTS

PREFACE

A few years ago R.T. Edwards, Inc., the publisher of the *Journal of Forensic Accounting*, and its Editor-in-Chief, D. Larry Crumbley, conceived the idea for a Special Supplement on expert witnessing to accompany the journal. Today, their idea is a reality. It is with genuine appreciation and deep gratitude for their vision and dedication to this work, and their confidence and trust in me to assist them, that I introduce you to *Expert Witnessing in Forensic Accounting*.

Included in this Supplement are eleven chapters written for the benefit of expert witnesses, consultants, and the attorneys that engage their services. The topics include advice on what to do and what not to do while testifying, how to succeed as an expert witness, roles of an accounting expert as witness and consultant, *Daubert* challenges, qualifying as an expert witness, understanding advocacy, working a case study, admonitions to counsel about timing and selection of expert witnesses, deposition and cross-examination strategies, and familiarity with privileged information and communications.

Many years ago, under cross-examination while engaged as an expert witness for the defense, it occurred to me how very effective the federal prosecutor was at having me testify on behalf of the government! He knew I would answer every question truthfully no matter who was asking. As an attorney that had thoroughly prepared for cross-examination of an opposing expert, he inquired about my reputation and prior testimony. During his preparation for cross-examination, he would have learned beforehand, for example, that four criminal defense attorneys, who aggressively grilled me almost a decade earlier for six hours one day before a federal judge, failed to convince the judge that I allegedly violated the grand jury secrecy rule 6(e) while I was an IRS agent. As a result of obtaining background information about me from prosecutors, government agents and defense attorneys, he learned that I would respond truthfully to questions no matter who was asking or what the question. He skillfully made me his expert witness too.

The preceding story reminds us that experts must tell the truth. More than a reminder, it permeates all that we do. It establishes our reputation, credibility and effectiveness. Our knowledge, skill, training and education can never substitute for our good name. Telling the truth is one of several commandments for expert witnesses to faithfully follow. This is where we begin your Supplement – with integrity. From here, you will learn to challenge assumptions, to pay attention to details, to refrain from advocacy, to gain confidence, to qualify as an expert, to know your client's attorney, to prepare for testimony and to succeed as an expert. We end the supplement with a philosophical discussion about *Daubert*. It brings us full circle to where we started – with integrity.

As you read through the chapters, you will get practical and timely advice from very experienced accounting experts, practitioners and educators who have taken the time to share their thoughts with you. They have joined together with one message in mind – to help you become better at what you do. Successful experts do not work in a vacuum. We learn from each other and benefit from our mistakes. And often, we should listen to what others have to say and contribute to their success as well as our own by exchanging ideas, sharing experiences and encouraging discourse among us. This is the central theme of *Expert Witnessing in Forensic Accounting*. It is a learning experience to benefit from and to enjoy.

Walter J. Pagano
Guest Editor and Contributor
April 2005

CHAPTER 1

The 10 Commandments for Expert Witnesses

Dana Basney

HERE ARE THE TOP 10 TIPS FOR EXPERT WITNESSES:

1. Tell the truth – be an expert, not an advocate.

There is nothing more compelling than the truth, and it usually seems to come out in trial. It is the attorney's job to be an advocate for the client, not yours. Most effective expert testimony is factual and supported by logic, not emotion. The expert's job is to base his opinion on an unbiased view of the facts, and then to be an advocate for his opinion, not an advocate for the client. The more the trier of fact sees you as a client advocate, the less effective your testimony will be. Recently, I had a divorce case in which I was charged with determining the respondent's income available for support. I started with the tax return and made appropriate adjustments, explaining the reason for those adjustments to the court. The income I derived was significantly higher than what my client had shown in his income and expense declaration due to the add-backs I made to income. The opposition expert appeared to ignore the law in many areas, counting proceeds from loans as income available for support, imputing income from the individual's retirement accounts and imputing income

Dana Basney, MSBA, CPA, CVA, CIRA is shareholder in the public accounting firm of Mayer Hoffman McCann P.C., and a Director of the Litigation and Insolvency Support Services Group CBIZ - Nation Smith Hermes Diamond, in San Diego, California.

This article is from the Litigation and Support Services Group at CBIZ-Nation Smith Hermes Diamond. It contains useful and pragmatic information for experts in business litigation.

based on the value of the respondents home, to arrive at a very large number. The court, when asked why it adopted my position rather than my opposition's, responded, "In reading the Basney declarations, I find them to be both well reasoned, credible and consistent with the facts indicated to have been relied upon." The court went on to state that the opposing experts opinion" seems more advocacy that credible expert opinion." One sanity check I use when I draft a declaration is to pretend that the opposing party in the case hired you. I ask myself would my testimony be different? If the answer is yes, I revisit the opinions I express and try to get back on track.

2. Don't overstate your credentials or experience. Academic credentials are important, but the trier of fact will be far more impressed with the logic and common sense you use in coming to your conclusions than your credentials.

Although it is important to understand the theory of accounting, it is equally or more important to have had practical experience in the field and to be able to express that knowledge in a logical and concise manner.

Practical knowledge of the industry, business operations, accounting procedures, how paperwork flows within a business, how a business operates, and the interrelationships between income and expense, and cash flow and income is invaluable.

The most important job of the accounting expert is to teach and inform the jury or the court. If the jury understands the expert's opinions, no matter how simply put, you will get a much more favorable result than trying to get them to accept an opinion they don't understand.

Many novice experts think that juries are somehow going to be overwhelmed by their credentials into accepting their opinions; in reality most juries don't care much about credentials. They are more concerned with understanding the basis and the logic of your opinions.

In my experience academicians tend to be poor expert witnesses because they often have problems relating their testimony to real world situations. An ounce of common sense, expressed is a straightforward manner, is worth a ton of credentials.

3. Check on your opposing expert's credentials with the State Board of Accountancy or other appropriate agency.

Unfortunately, there are experts who don't abide by the Second Commandment above and will overstate their credentials. Always check on the opposing expert's credentials with the State Board of Accountancy. It is not unheard of for people seeking work as experts to overstate their credentials. Check your opposition's professional credentials and references.

In one case I had against the Internal Revenue Service, the opposing expert stated he was a CPA. Having checked his credentials with the State Board of Accountancy, I had obtained a letter from the Board stating that the individual in question was not licensed in California and could not represent himself as a CPA. After getting the opposing expert to state he was a CPA on at least five occasions in cross examination, the lawyer for my client entered into evidence the letter I had obtained from the State Board of Accountancy. After reading the letter the judge leaned toward the unfortunate expert who was still in the witness box and stated, "Sir, you are dealing with federal prosecutors here, you might want to think about taking the Fifth Amendment." Needless to say this didn't help either his client's case or his own career.

In reality, this individual had previously been a licensed CPA for a number of years before he let his license expire three months prior to trial for not keeping current on his continuing education requirement. Had he simply stated that he had been a licensed practicing CPA for many years and had recently let his license lapse because he was too busy to keep up his continuing education requirement, and was slightly delinquent in getting it renewed, nobody on the jury would really have cared. But this individual ignored the Second Commandment above and met with devastating results. In that case the jury was out less than ten minutes when they asked the judge if they could award more money than the taxes my client was suing the government to recover. My client got in excess of $200,000 in fees and costs from the government under the provisions of the taxpayer Bill of Rights in addition to the taxes he was suing to recover.

4. Never let attorneys feed you selective information that screens out information that may be adverse to your client.

Be sure you get all the facts that are pertinent to your testimony. Unfortunately some inexperienced lawyers will try to shape your testimony by giving you only selected facts, which could only lead to one conclusion. Be sure you get all the facts. If you don't get all the facts needed to form a proper opinion, it will only come out at trial and your testimony will be discredited. It will be your reputation that suffers, not the attorney's if you don't get all the facts and are ambushed at trial. Often adverse facts can be minimized by putting them in perspective or by explaining them. Adverse facts should never be ignored, however.

5. Maintain controls over the documents from the very beginning. Always reference your work papers to show where all your data comes from, but never write notes to the file.

Business litigation cases tend to be document intensive. I have had cases with literally millions of documents. It is extremely important to establish a document referencing system as soon as possible in the case. A common referencing system with each document being *Bates* stamped greatly facilitates the efficient handling of the case and communications between the expert and legal counsel. Request that counsel *Bates Stamp* and index all documents before giving them to you. A good document control system will keep both the expert and the attorney from spending dozens of hours searching for records.

It is also very important to reference the source of all the information, numbers and statistics that you use in your report. Even though you may be aware of the source of the information when you do the work, it may be months between the time that you do the work and you are deposed on it. In some cases trials are appealed and remanded for retrial. I have had cases in which I have testified in court several years after having done the work supporting my opinions. There is no way that I could remember the source of all the underlying data used to form my opinion over such a long period. Because the file was referenced in great detail, I did not have to rely on memory.

Once, I attended an opposing expert's deposition where the opposing expert could not reconstruct a key calculation, which formed the crux of his testimony. He was forced to go on the record stating that he did not understand where he got the data that went into his calculation and therefore he could not explain his own calculation. Needless to say a motion to exclude his testimony was drafted before the ink on his deposition had even dried. Had he referenced the source of his raw data and how it went into his calculation, he might not have gotten into his predicament.

Most CPAs with audit experience are quite used to referencing work papers, which makes them well suited to working on litigation matters. Most auditors, however, suffer from a compulsion to document their every thought and justify their every action in the work papers. This can prove to be disastrous. If you have 1,000 lines of notes and documentation explaining your position in the file, you can be assured that the opposing counsel is not going to compliment you for having such a well documented file while he is examining you. You can also be assured that he will only ask you about the one sentence in a thousand that can be misconstrued, taken out of context, or is ambiguous enough to be used against you. If you write notes documenting all the files that you have requested, you will not be complimented for your thoroughness. Instead you will be asked about the single innocuous document that you requested in writing but did not get. That document will become the most important document in the case on cross-examination.

It is best not to write any notes in the file for the above reasons.

Perhaps the most damaging note I ever saw in a case was where the opposing experts lead schedule had a note written diagonally across it, which stated, "This makes no (expletive deleted) sense." When asked what the note said, the expert turned beet red and professed he could not read it. We immediately had the exhibit blown up to a 3 foot by 5 foot size! Unfortunately the case settled before we could present it to the jury.

In another embarrassing situation, I was working with a very experienced and competent audit manager for the first time. I gave him my usual admonishment about not making any notes in the file. Shortly before my deposition I reviewed the file. The first page of the file contained a note written by this audit manager, which stated "Do not take any notes, and do not put any notes in the file." As I said earlier auditors tend to be compulsive about such things!

6. Bring out the weak points in your testimony during direct examination

The opposition is sure to bring up these weaknesses in its cross examination. By beating them to the punch, you show that you were aware of these weaknesses and have considered them in forming your opinions. Discussing the weaknesses in your case gives you a chance to explain their significance and to put them in perspective. It is rare to have a lawsuit where there are not some facts adverse to your client's position. If the adverse facts are not brought out in your direct exam and put into perspective, they will only be brought out by the opposition expert and blown out of all perspective.

Some lawyers may be opposed to doing this, as they do not want to bring any unfavorable facts to the attention of the jury. Remember it is your reputation that will be damaged when the opposing expert brings out these facts and puts them in the worse possible light. It is always better to steal the other side's thunder in the context of your own testimony.

7. Always use visual displays in presenting your testimony.

Educators will tell you that the vast majority of the population processes visual information much more readily than oral information. In the courtroom there is much to be said in favor of the old adage "One picture is worth a thousand words." The use of Exhibits is very important in getting your message to the trier of fact. Despite the overwhelming evidence regarding the value of visual displays from the educational and psychological communities, amazingly some experts merely pontificate from the stand. It really doesn't matter if they are correct or incorrect in their opinions, because the jury is probably not listening after the first few minutes. Whether we like to admit it or not, accounting testimony is usually not very titillating and it does not grab most peoples attention. A proper visual display can help keep the trier of fact focused on your testimony. I always try to use large exhibit boards that allow me to demonstrate the steps I've used in doing my calculations. If the jury can follow the process and procedures you have used, they are much more likely to accept your number over that of the pontificator who merely states his conclusion without explanation.

Sometimes a visual display can be very dramatic and is virtually irrefutable. Once I had a client who purchased a very large and luxurious home, only to discover that it had a water seepage problem. I calculated my client's damages using two approaches. The first approach was to calculate the cost to repair the damage. The second approach, which was based on the rescission of the purchase agreement, took the sum that the client was paying for his former, more modest home, and subtracted that from the cost of maintaining the new water damaged home, as well as refunding the monies invested to buy the home. In my examination after I presented this calculation, opposing counsel asked me why I didn't reduce my calculation by the amount that the rental value of the new, much larger and more luxurious home, was in excess of the rental value of the previous more modest residence. I responded by pointing to an exhibit, which had a large blow up of a photo showing mushrooms growing up through the living room carpet of the home in question and explaining that I was unable to get rental comps for homes with mushrooms growing through their living room carpet! The case settled immediately after the deposition, to a large part based on that single picture that made it impossible to deny that there was a major water problem in the home.

8. Never personally attack an opposition expert in your testimony.

In personally attacking an opposing expert witness you are far more likely to create sympathy for him or her and animosity toward you and your client than to help your case.

Juries recognize that by directing your attack at the individual rather than the expert's opinions implies that you cannot attack those opinions. Remember it is the expert's opinions that you have to attack, not the expert.

I recently had a case where my testimony was limited to opining on the accounting principles, which were relevant to the matter at hand. In order to save cost, my client used a non-CPA to trace certain transactions, which formed the actual core of the damages that my clients suffered.

The opposing party was a large insurance conglomerate with an unlimited budget, which hired a very experienced CPA to present their side of the case. The experienced expert went out of his way to point out that his opposing expert was not a CPA and to address his credentials, or lack of them, rather than his testimony. This did not sit well with the jury who liked the less credentialed expert and who understood his testimony because he presented it in a straightforward manner. It caused a backlash against the opposition's expert. The opposition expert would have been far more effective had he addressed his less credentialed opponent's testimony rather than his credentials. Attacking opposing expert's credentials, bias, or experience is best left for the attorneys to do in oral argument; it only cheapens an expert's testimony to do so. Stick to the opposition's opinions, not his qualifications. It will be obvious to the jury how his qualifications compare to yours when each side examines their expert's qualifications, as is customarily done as part of his direct exam.

9. Encourage your clients to bring you into a case as early as possible

As an accounting expert you will often have unique knowledge that can help in discovery. You can help to identify documents that should exist and can be used to refute the opposition. Some lawyers will bring in the expert at the last minute to save fees. This can be disastrous when you are brought in after discovery is closed and you find out that the lawyer failed to ask for the documents you will need to form your opinion.

Accountants can be invaluable in helping to direct discovery in a case. From their auditing, tax, and litigation backgrounds, they are usually aware of the types of documents that companies and individuals maintain. Cases, which may have thousands of documents, are often won or lost based on a few key documents, the so-called "Smoking Guns." Accountants can assist in making discovery requests that are specific enough to bring these "Smoking Guns" to light.

Accounting experts are also problem solvers. Oftimes a review of the damages and the ability to collect those damages prior to filing litigation can save the client hundreds of thousands of dollars in legal fees and result in an early settlement or reconsideration of the merits of the litigation. Accountants are invaluable in analyzing the costs and merits of litigation as well as alternatives to litigation.

10. If you are unsure of what your testimony may be, try to get hired first as a consultant for the client's attorney. Then, if your testimony proves not to be favorable – it will be shielded from discovery by the attorney consultant privilege. Never be afraid not to take a case.

Many cases are fairly straight forward, such as determining damages from lost wages, which is usually more of an exercise in math than an exercise in judgment. Other cases, such as those cases involving what constitutes the proper accounting for complex transactions, are more involved and you will usually not be able to give an opinion on such cases until after you have done an extensive review of the pertinent facts. Upon doing such a review, it is entirely possible that your opinion may in fact be adverse to the party that hired you. If you are hired by the client's counsel as a consultant, your adverse opinion will be protected from discovery. Once you are designated as an expert, you may have to disclose an adverse opinion to the detriment of your client's case.

If you are honest and professional in your testimony, you will eventually have a case where your opinions are more favorable to the opposing side than your own client. If you are hired as a consultant you can still do a big service for your client by showing him the weakness in his position and encouraging him to save the cost of trial by entering into a settlement early in the case.

Not every client you will be asked to represent will be descended purely from the angels. Sometimes you will need to acknowledge wrongdoings by your client, if you are to give honest testimony. Often these wrongdoings can be put in perspective. If your client refuses to accept that some of your testimony may be adverse to him, then you might want to consider leaving the case. Your reputation is your greatest asset; don't sacrifice it to please a client. You will get other clients, you only have one reputation, and without a good reputation you are of no benefit to any client.

CHAPTER 2

How To Succeed as an Expert Witness

David Nolte

Expert witnesses are more important than ever. Most complicated cases do not settle until after the experts have issued comprehensive reports or had their depositions taken. This trend will increase because education has not kept pace with the continuing increase in knowledge, causing an ever-widening gap between what the average person knows and what specialists know.

Serving as an expert witness is a difficult job. The attorney's job is also daunting, but selecting an experienced witness will make that challenging task much easier. This article is written to help the expert witness, but the same advice will also help the employing attorney get a better result.

PLANNING SOWS THE SEEDS OF SUCCESS

You and your employing lawyer should outline the analytical procedures to be performed, the estimated cost, and the expected schedule. Identify key records needed for your work, including those from your client's opponent. Factor in delays for discovery battles involving critical records. Reach agreement regarding how much time the analyses will require. Regardless of the reason for not receiving materials timely, you cannot produce good work instantaneously after receiving information.

David Nolte is a principal at Fulcrum Financial Inquiry LLP. He has 30 years experience performing forensic accounting, auditing, business appraisals, and related financial consulting. He regularly serves as an expert witness. Fulcrum's website address is www.fulcruminquiry.com.

Make sure you understand how your opinions fit into the general argument of the case. Understand the time line of key events in the case and their consequences. In complex litigation, there are often multiple key dates that an expert needs to address. To avoid reworking conclusions and flawed analyses, ensure that you are using data that is pertinent to those dates.

Avoid the ever-present temptation to accept additional responsibility in areas in which you are not truly qualified. If you are discredited in some area that you are covering as "a favor," you will also lose credibility in the more important areas of your true expertise.

ANALYSIS BRINGS RESULTS

You will almost certainly be discredited if you do not adhere to the analytical rigors of your profession. Your conclusions should be supported with analysis, testing, and inspection. Descriptions beginning with phrases such as "I saw," "I heard," and "I examined" should constitute the strongest support for the conclusions. Judges and juries are less persuaded by summaries beginning with "in my opinion" or "based on my experience" than they are by more positive phrases such as "my analysis indicates," "the data supports" or "the market tells us."

Consider whether there is government data or studies that corroborate your position. Government information is often highly credible to a judge or jury. So-called learned treatises or academic publications are not as useful. These works are as numerous and varied as the experts who prepare them. If you find a learned treatise that supports your argument, you can probably also find another treatise by an equally qualified author that conflicts with your position.

If there is more than one expert working on the same case, arrange to meet with your employing attorney in a joint conference. The experts should discuss their methodology and tentative conclusions with one another. Many litigators avoid this because the meeting is subject to discovery. While unfavorable disclosure is a risk, the greater problem is having your multiple experts impeach one another with inconsistent testimony.

Well before reaching your final conclusions, meet with the employing attorney to explain how your work is progressing. These meetings should discuss the good news and the not-so-good news. Be willing to explain:

1. Favorable and unfavorable facts

2. Available testing methods to address potential challenges

3. False or weak assumptions in your analysis, or other inadequate work

4. Opinions upon which reasonable experts may differ, and

5. Possible "long shots" that might be worth the effort to investigate.

BE PREPARED TO ANSWER PREDICTABLE BUT DIFFICULT QUESTIONS

Actually, the questions are never difficult ... it's the answers that provide a challenge. You should have answers for questions that elicit limitations in, or concerns with, your work. Examples include:

1. What assumptions did you make?

2. What is the factual basis for this opinion, and how do these facts lead to your conclusion?

3. What information have you relied on that was provided by counsel or your client?

4. What concerns do you have regarding your conclusions?

5. Under what circumstances would you use a different methodology?

6. What alternative hypotheses could explain what you observed?

7. What other work would you have liked to have performed?

Hypothetical questions also provide a challenge. Hypothetical questions can be used to move you and your client off the established story that you came prepared to present. Hypothetical questions can turn you into your opponent's witness when a different set of facts are presented. The key in answering these hazardous questions is to be sure that the hypothetical question (i) is complete (i.e., not missing any key information that might change the answer), and (ii) is based on circumstances that are realistic and therefore subject to a meaningful response.

To avoid accidentally supporting your opponent's case, you will need to understand other issues that indirectly relate to your testimony. The fact that you were not hired to address a particular subject does not prevent your client's opponent from asking you questions about that subject. Because of your employing lawyer's familiarity with the dispute, he will usually not appreciate the difficulty that you will face with these surprise attacks. Your preparation for the deposition by the employing attorney should include specific warning about these matters, including related hypothetical questions.

GRAPHICALLY PRESENT YOUR CONCLUSIONS

Your work is not complete until it is supported with demonstrative charts, graphs, or other visually appealing exhibits. You may have the best conclusion and credentials but may lose in the courtroom to someone who has prepared a presentation that is more intuitive and easier to understand.

Studies consistently show that memory increases 700 percent when the information is both explained and shown. We know the truth of the adages, "A picture is worth a thousand words" and "Seeing is believing." Armed with this knowledge, you should improve your presentation with graphics.

Remember "Show & Tell" in kindergarten? These inexperienced presenters naturally place their emphasis, not on themselves, but on the object that they are showing. By focusing attention on the evidence and away from a witness's self-consciousness, a presentation improves dramatically. This is true for both expert and lay witnesses.

In addition to improving information retention and improving your presentation, graphics (i) enhance the jury's attention span, (ii) increase witness credibility, and (iii) forcefully communicate how your opinion relates to other witnesses. If allowed in the jury room, your graphics will also be a tool that can be used by sympathetic jurors to convince the others.

Here is how to create successful graphics:

1. **Keep it simple** - This is the rule most frequently violated. Too much information in a visual aid will confuse rather than clarify. Creativity does not mean complication. To achieve your goal, invoke the following guidelines:

   - Each chart should have only one major point. Use multiple charts that build on one another for more complex ideas.

   - Details that are too small to be easily seen should be eliminated from the chart. If necessary, create a second (and simple) chart.

   - Eliminate extra words, numbers, and details. They will not be remembered anyway.

2. **Create the graphics yourself** - You can not be considered a superior and experienced trial expert until you can draft your conclusions graphically. The advantages of drafting your own graphics include:

   - It is usually less costly, because you are already familiar with the entire effort.

   - The graphics will be more faithful to your methodology.

   - You will be more confident and convincing because of having been personally involved with the creation of the graphics.

3. **Improve interest through variety** - Blow-ups of written documents by themselves will cause a jury to lose interest almost as fast as if no graphics are used. Use a combination of illustrations, photographs, pie charts, line charts, bar charts, document blow-ups, and video. Display these through a variety of presentation methods, such as foam boards, models, and on-screen projection.

Variety also means not using graphics for everything. Although you should always have some graphic support, you need to select issues that deserve illustration. Visual reinforcement tells the jury that this is something worth remembering. Select issues and ideas that are truly important, and direct graphic attention there.

4. **Test your charts with those unfamiliar with your case** - You need to be able to explain the key facts and rationale of each of your graphics in a few minutes. If your graphic is unable to be immediately understood by those unfamiliar with your case, then your explanation and/or your graphic needs to be reworked. Your jury will not have studied your case in the agonizing detail that you have. The risk is that what is obvious to you will be lost on your judge or jury.

This does not require expensive jury research, although such research will certainly also be helpful. The small budget case can be reviewed with colleagues and coworkers who promise to be painfully candid in their assessments.

5. **Use only properly-scaled and labeled color graphs** - All presentations must be accurately scaled to show amounts, measures, times, etc. For example, the y-axis (the vertical line in any numerical chart) should begin with zero, and not skip any amounts through the data that is being shown. Doing otherwise presents a biased picture of how much the graphed data is increasing or decreasing.

Almost every case benefits from a graphical timeline to accurately track key events. Timelines are effective in telling your side of the story by proving or disproving liability, motive, and damages. As with any graphic showing data, the timeline should have an accurate scale.

Use color to (i) facilitate and simplify the labels on your charts, and (ii) unify related items within a chart or between charts. Doing so will make your charts intuitive and more simple.

Your charts should include a source of the information that it conveys. This improves credibility and will cause the chart to serve as a reminder of key evidence.

6. **Use word charts rarely, if at all** - Not all graphics are created equal. Graphics need to show pictures, concepts, and objects – not words and numbers. A typical "PowerPoint" slide presentation consisting of words and bullet points lacks creativity and interest. Spreadsheets with numbers are even worse. Simply displaying words and numbers will not do anything to make your presentation memorable or persuasive.

7. **Remember the seriousness of the setting** - Modern computerized graphics packages have a wide range of clip art, animation, flash movements, and other fancy do-das. That does not mean you need to use them in a courtroom. Sometimes, the most expensive graphics are not the most effective.

Juries have a job to do, and most of them take it seriously. Keep to the basics. Numbers should be presented with simple pie, bar, and line charts. Animations that show how something works are effective, but stay away from animations that show moving objects simply to dress up the presentation.

Overuse of superfluous graphic design elements may make your presentation entertaining, but it will not make it persuasive. The added elements may even backfire by raising the suspicion that you are attempting to hide something by being slick.

8. **Charts improve the entire process** - Graphics can be useful during settlement, witness preparation, and strategy planning, so develop graphics early in the process. For example, schematics, timelines and other charts that present facts can be used during depositions as a means of having other witnesses agree with your presentation of the facts.

Each time you present your graphics, you will need to consider presentation logistics. This is particularly true in courtrooms, where the placement of the judge, jury, and courtroom furniture may limit your presentation options. See the actual layout where your presentation will occur before finalizing your plans.

RETAIN CREDIBILITY AND INDEPENDENCE

Remember that you are there to support your specific opinion(s), not to present your client's entire case. Experts should explain and defend their options, and their opinions can certainly favor their client. However, you must maintain the attitude and appearance of being an independent servant of the court. If you show unwillingness to acknowledge an obvious favorable point of your opponent or to admit the possibility of a reasonable alternate view, you fail the credibility test.

Chapter 3

Perspectives of an Accounting Expert as an Expert Consultant and Testifying Witness

Walter J. Pagano

INTRODUCTION

The first two articles in this supplement give an overview of the essential attributes that an expert witness should have, and make important recommendations to succeed as an expert witness. In addition to the knowledge, skill, training and education expected of an expert, an accounting expert's professional engagement experiences complete the foundation that is essential to rendering consulting advice to attorneys and their clients or opinion testimony to a trier of fact in a legal forum. An expert accounting consultant or witness draws upon this 'foundation of expertise' to provide independent and objective advice and opinions no matter whose side the expert represents. In any litigation matter involving accounting, financial or tax issues, although the roles of the accounting expert may differ in terms of the sought after outcome depending on whether the expert is retained by the plaintiff's or defendant's counsel or by a prosecutor, both experts are examining the same financial information and have access to the same discovery. Although there may be differences in opinion about interpreting financial "facts" or applying accounting or tax principles to them, there will be one body of sufficient credible evidential matter that both sides rely on in forming opinions. Experts must be fair, impartial, and reasonable regardless of the side they represent. If they are, then the differences in their opinions should narrow.

Walter J. Pagano, CPA, CFE, DABFA is a legal support services partner at Eisner LLP with over 30 years forensic accounting experience specializing in analyzing accounting and financial records in civil and criminal matters, including internal investigations, white-collar crime, and tax investigations and controversies.

Plaintiff or prosecution experts examine financial information to obtain facts and circumstances that are favorable to and support their theory of the case, while defense experts examine the same set of financial information for facts and circumstances that support defenses that demonstrate why the plaintiff or prosecutor are arguably wrong or, notwithstanding, that the amount of damages, tax loss or business value is different from the amount alleged. Although the experts' roles are different, experts must remember that their reputations and credibility are "on trial" and subject to public scrutiny from the moment that they agree to be an expert consultant or witness. Experts who advocate for clients positions that do not have a sufficient basis in the facts, whose work product is not founded on reliable principles and methods, or who wrongly apply principles and methods, will not be sought after by the bench and bar to educate and assist the trier of fact to understand the evidence or to determine a fact in issue, or for any other role.

ROLES FOR THE ACCOUNTANT

Although there are many roles for the expert accountant to have based on his or her expertise, essentially the expert accountant will work either as an expert consultant or expert witness. Generally, if it is counsel's intent to retain the expert accountant as a consultant, then the accountant is retained as an agent for the attorney and is cloaked with the attorney-client privilege. See *United States v. Kovel*, 296 F.2d 918 (2d Cir. 1961). At the beginning of an engagement, most counsel usually retains the accountant as a consultant until such time as a decision is made to name the accountant as an expert witness. This allows for the free exchange of confidential information and opinions without inadvertently waiving the attorney-client privilege. However, once the accountant is named as an expert witness and eventually testifies at deposition or trial, the attorney-client privilege generally no longer applies. So, if it is counsel's intent to retain an accountant as an expert testifying witness, then the accountant generally is not cloaked with the attorney-client privilege and therefore, the accountant's work product is discoverable. There are instances when counsel has successfully argued that certain information that an expert witness has may come within the privilege notwithstanding that he or she testifies.

Roles for the Accountant as an Expert Consultant

When counsel retains an accountant as an expert consultant, the law firm and accountant execute a "Kovel" letter. This letter sets forth essential elements that establish the attorney-client privilege between the client, law firm and accountant. Although the form of the letter may vary from firm to firm, generally the essential elements of the letter include that the accountant 1) works under the attorney's direction and reports directly to counsel in order to assist the attorney in providing legal advice to the client, 2) will not disclose to anyone, without prior written permission, the nature or content of any oral or written communication, nor any information gained from the inspection of any record or document submitted to him or her, nor will he or she permit inspection of any papers or documents without the attorney's prior written permission, 3) will hold all workpapers, records or other documents that he or she prepares or obtains solely for counsel's convenience and subject to counsel's unqualified right to instruct him or her with respect to possession and control and 4) will immediately notify counsel of any events such as a request for the production of any documents or records covered by the Kovel arrangement. It is very important to know that the *Kovel* privilege does not apply to situations when the attorney is providing advice such as accounting or investment advice rather than legal advice to a client.

There are many cases when counsel may retain an accounting expert as a consultant. Among these cases are internal investigations, white-collar crime, civil or criminal tax, breach of contract, shareholder disputes, recovery of damages for fraud, recovery of damages for lost profits, assessing commercial damages, matrimonial, professional conduct, GAAP and GAAS. Accounting experts testify in all legal forums, are court appointed as experts, monitors, special fiscal agents and examiners.

As an expert consultant, an accountant usually performs many roles and tasks that may overlap with those of an expert witness. Before beginning an engagement, an accounting expert should first undertake a conflict search. Once conflicts have been cleared, it is important for the accountant to understand the theory of the case and the part that he or she will play. For example, a stock purchase agreement may include financial, tax and accounting representations and warranties that one party alleges have been breached. In this situation, the accountant may be called upon to determine whether 1) financial statements are in accordance with the company's books and records, 2) financial statements have been prepared in conformity with GAAP, and 3) financial statements present fairly the results of operations of the company.

The expert accountant's role in this situation will be a forensic accountant. Generally, the term 'forensic accountant' refers to an accountant applying accounting principles or standards to a dispute in a legal forum such as in a court of law or at an arbitration hearing. The forensic accountant takes the financial facts obtained during discovery and applies them to the legal issues or problems that counsel is litigating in order to form an opinion whether there are breaches in the financial and accounting representations and warranties referred to in the preceding paragraph. Therefore, in this illustration, the role of the forensic accountant is to apply accounting principles or standards to transactions that have previously been reported for financial statement purposes that are now the subject of a legal proceeding.

Another role that an expert accountant may have is a fraud auditor. Assume, for example, that a company's audit committee wants to be active in detecting and preventing fraud. It may decide to retain accountants to detect fraudulent behavior by reviewing operations in addition to processes and to establish policies and procedures to prevent fraud. In some cases, if fraudulent behavior is already suspected, the company will first retain a law firm in order for the accountants to work as consultants for the law firm and be cloaked with the attorney-client privilege. The accountant's role now changes to conducting an internal investigation under the direction of counsel.

Depending on the specific facts and circumstances, the theory of the case and the expert accountant's role, the accountant's services may include, but are not limited to 1) reviewing and analyzing books, records and transactions; 2) researching accounting and tax issues; 3) interviewing; 4) examining the outside accountant's or auditor's workpapers; 5) educating counsel; 6) in a government investigation, reviewing the government's theory of the case, computations and meeting with the government's experts and 7) assisting the attorney to depose or cross-examine witnesses.

Usually in criminal investigations conducted by FBI, IRS, SEC or Postal Inspectors, forensic accountants are consultants retained under the *Kovel* privilege. If a trial is likely, defense counsel may retain another expert accountant who will testify at trial. The reason is that the expert consultant will most likely have privileged information and work product that counsel would not want subject to cross-examination.

THE ACCOUNTANT AS AN EXPERT WITNESS

An accountant testifies as an expert witness at a deposition and at trial. The material discussed above pertaining to the accountant as an expert consultant applies equally to the expert witness. The obvious difference between the two experts is the consultant may not be an expert witness in a particular case; whereas the expert witness is also an expert consultant who advises counsel about matters central to his or her expert report and testimony.

Counsel retains an expert accounting witness to review information and documents, to assist counsel in rendering legal advice to the client and to offer opinion testimony at trial. The expert's opinions are usually in the form of a written report. Federal Rules of Civil Procedure ("FRCP"), section 26, relating to General Provisions Governing Discovery, Duty of Disclosure, provides in FRCP 26(a)(2), Disclosure of Expert Testimony, the following:

1. Written report prepared and signed by the witness.

2. Written report shall contain a complete statement of all opinions to be expressed; the basis and reasons therefore; the data or other information considered by the witness in forming the opinion.

3. Exhibits.

4. Qualifications of the witness, including publications authored within preceding ten years.

5. Compensation.

6.   Listing of any other cases in which the witness has testified as an expert at trial or by deposition within the preceding four years.

Counsel retains an expert accounting witness who will offer opinion testimony at trial to help a judge or jury understand certain financial, accounting or tax aspects of the case. The expert accountant's testimony is the opinion evidence that counsel introduces at trial in order for the judge and jury to understand "scientific, technical, or other specialized knowledge" that usually a fact or lay witness is unable to offer. Experience tells us that in order for the judge and jury to understand the specialized knowledge associated with the case, the expert testifying witness must be able to teach and educate them. In cases that involve accounting, financial and tax issues which include many areas of specialized knowledge such as generally accepted accounting principles, generally accepted auditing standards, tax law, Sarbanes-Oxley, corporate governance, compliance and controversy, the expert accounting witness must explain and define for the trier of fact unfamiliar concepts and words in easy to understand language. To the extent possible, the expert witness must avoid using technical language and consider using graphics to make his or her thoughts and ideas not only easy to understand but also credible, convincing and memorable for the trier of fact.

An expert accounting witness communicates opinions at deposition or at trial during direct examination and cross-examination by articulating the reasons for the opinions and the facts and data that support them. The expert's opinions are also his or her message or theme stated throughout the report as well as while testifying. Therefore, in order for the expert witness to communicate the message or theme while giving testimony, he or she should state as often as possible conclusions and opinions supported with data and facts.

While testifying, there are some basic tenets to remember. They are 1) tell the truth, 2) focus and concentrate, 3) do not volunteer, 4) listen to and answer 'the' question, 5) respect the deposing or cross-examining attorney, 6) be certain, 7) know your professional standards, 8) listen to objections, 9) do not guess or speculate, 10) prepare thoroughly and completely and again, (11) focus and concentrate.

I know from my own personal experiences that focusing and concentrating at all times while testifying are as important as telling the truth and listening to the question. At times, however, these can be difficult tasks – especially over several days of testifying. We are human. We can make mistakes. However, I have been very fortunate over the years to have worked with very talented attorneys who do not hesitate to continually reinforce and repeat how important it is to focus and concentrate. I genuinely appreciate this advice and when I hear it often from counsel, I know that I am working with a very talented, concerned and knowledgeable professional. It is a professionally prepared attorney who thoroughly prepares his lay and expert witnesses for trial and who reinforces these very important tenets, as well as discusses the rules of evidence with experts.

FEDERAL RULES OF EVIDENCE ("FRE")

There are 5 Federal Rules of Evidence that specifically apply to testimony given by experts. The rules are found in FRE 702 to 706.

1. Rule 702, related to Testimony by Experts, opens the door for individuals having specialized knowledge to assist the trier of fact to understand the evidence presented at trial or to determine a fact in issue during the trial. Usually, counsel will offer to the court an individual as an expert once he or she is 'qualified' as expert after *voie dire.*

2. Rule 703, related to Bases of Opinion Testimony by Experts, allows an expert to base his or her opinion on facts or data perceived by the expert or made known to the expert at or before the hearing. Opposing counsel may challenge whether the expert in the particular field or discipline reasonably relied on the facts and data. In ruling on this objection, the trial court weighs the probative value of the information against its prejudicial effect.

3. Rule 704, related to Opinion on Ultimate Issue, provides for an expert to offer an opinion on an ultimate issue to be decided by judge or jury. It does not, however, allow an expert to testify with

respect to the mental state or condition of a defendant in a criminal case.

4.   Rule 705, related to Disclosure of Facts or Data Underlying Expert Opinion, allows an expert to offer an opinion supported by his or her reasons without first testifying to the underlying facts or data for the opinion. Usually, opposing counsel on cross-examination will require the expert to disclose the underlying facts or data.

5.   Rule 706, related to Court Appointed Experts, provides for a court to appoint an expert on its own or on the motion of any party.

THE GATEKEEPER

Although Rule 702 opens the door for expert testimony, opposing counsel can easily challenge it. Judges, as the gatekeepers, have often closed the door, thus not allowing the expert testimony of some individuals. Experts should become familiar with the many challenges made by opposing counsel to exclude their testimony. *Daubert, Target* and *Kumho Tire* are very important to the expert testifying witness because, beginning with *Daubert*, they set the standard for allowing or not allowing the expert to testify at trial. Simply stated, *Daubert* and its progeny require that the expert testifying witness 1) has credentials to qualify as an expert, 2) has a basis in fact to support his or her testimony, 3) has reliable and relevant testimony and 4) has used generally accepted theories or techniques. The next article provides a more extensive discussion of this issue.

CONCLUSION

Accountants have specialized knowledge to assist the trier of fact to understand the evidence or to determine a fact in issue. This is their role as an expert testifying witness. As expert consultants, accountants assist counsel to understand the documents and information, accounting principles, auditing standards, financial concepts and tax law. Expert consultants retained by counsel are usually referred to as *Kovel* accountants because they are cloaked with the attorney-client privilege. Regardless of the accountant's roles, experts must be fair, reasonable and helpful in assisting counsel in prosecuting or defending a case because the trier of fact will place the greatest weight on the testimony of an expert who is credible and trustworthy.

An expert testifying witness must communicate in easy to understand words and ideas and explain the reasons that support his or her ultimate opinion. The expert witness should articulate his or her message or theme throughout deposition or trial testimony. Working with trial attorneys who thoroughly prepare their witnesses and remind them to remember basic expert testifying witness fundamentals are role models to follow and to learn from.

An expert witness must be familiar with the applicable Federal Rules of Civil Procedure, the Federal Rules of Evidence and the gatekeeper standards.

In the end, the expert witness must be helpful to the trier of fact.

CHAPTER 4

Accountants as Expert Witnesses: A Primer on Meeting Daubert Challenges

Bonita K. Peterson Kramer and **David R. Barnhill**

Accountants are often called to testify as expert witnesses in fraud trials or other legal disputes. Since *Daubert v. Merrell Dow Pharmaceuticals, Inc.* (1993), an increasing number of testifying experts have been subjected to challenges by opposing counsel in an attempt to prevent the experts from testifying. This article provides a background on the landmark case of *Daubert* and the related *Kumho Tire Company, Ltd. v. Patrick Carmichael* (1999) case, where the U.S. Supreme Court established standards for determining the admissibility of expert witness testimony. In addition, this article discusses a recent U.S. District Court case alleging tire failure, where defense counsel sought to exclude the plaintiff's expert witness from testifying under *Daubert*. In this decision, the plaintiff's expert witness was a nonscientific expert, as any accountant testifying as an expert would be classified. This decision supplies guidance about how to successfully meet *Daubert* challenges, which could be useful when an accountant is engaged to testify as an expert witness.

One axiom of fraud is "fraud is hidden" (Wells, 1998). By its very nature, fraud is concealed by the perpetrator in an attempt to avoid detection. Often, this concealment involves manipulation of the accounting records by the perpetrator, and depending upon the quality of the internal control

Bonita Peterson Kramer is professor of Accounting at Montana State University - Bozeman, Bozeman, Montana. David Barnhill is an attorney for the Montana Department of Public Health & Human Services. He is also a part-time adjunct instructor at the Helena Center of Technology of the University of Montana, where he currently teaches classes in ethics and employment law. This article originally appeared in the June 2003 issue of the *Journal of Forensic Accounting*.

system in place, it presents difficulty for investigators to determine the full extent of the fraud. Accountants – such as internal auditors, external auditors, or forensic auditors – play an important role by helping to unravel the fraud through their technical accounting knowledge and by helping the trier of fact to determine facts in issue. However, since *Daubert v. Merrell Dow Pharmaceuticals, Inc.* (1993), an increasing number of testifying experts in a variety of court cases have been challenged by opposing counsel in an attempt to prevent the experts from testifying. This article gives background information on the *Daubert* case and the related *Kumbo Tire Company, Ltd. v. Patrick Carmichael* (1999) case, where the U.S. Supreme Court established standards for determining the admissibility of expert witness testimony. In addition, this article discusses qualifying an expert witness, explains the underlying foundation behind a *Daubert* challenge, and provides guidance on how to successfully meet these challenges.

BACKGROUND

Daubert v. Merrell Dow Pharmaceuticals, Inc.

In June 1993, the U.S. Supreme Court delivered the opinion of *Daubert v. Merrell Dow Pharmaceuticals, Inc.* This dispute involved two minor children, Jason Daubert and Eric Schuller, both of whom were born with serious birth defects. They and their parents sued Merrell Dow Pharmaceuticals ("Dow") in California state court, alleging that the mothers' ingestion of Bendectin, an anti-nausea prescription drug marketed by Dow, caused the birth defects. Dow removed the suits to federal district court on the diversity grounds, subjecting administration of the cases to the Federal Rules of Evidence.

Dow moved for summary judgment, contending that Bendectin does not cause birth defects and the plaintiffs could not present any valid evidence to the contrary.[1] To support the motion for summary judgment, Dow submitted an affidavit from a well-credentialed expert, Dr. Steven H. Lamm, on the risks from exposure to various chemical substances. Dr. Lamm, a physician and epidemiologist, stated in his affidavit that he had reviewed more

---

[1] A motion for a summary judgement is a request by legal counsel for the court to rule that all or a part of the claim should be dismissed because there is no genuine issue of a material fact.

than 30 published studies on Bendectin and human birth defects, involving over 130,000 patients. Not one study had found evidence that Bendectin could cause malformations in human fetuses. As a result of his review of these studies, Dr. Lamm concluded that maternal use of Bendectin during the first trimester of pregnancy had not been shown to be a risk factor for human birth defects.

The plaintiffs did not dispute Dr. Lamm's summary of the published record regarding Bendectin. Rather, they produced testimony from eight experts of their own, all with impressive credentials. For example, one of the plaintiff's experts received his master's and doctorate degrees in chemistry from Columbia University and the University of Chicago, respectively, and was employed as a professor at New York Medical College, spending over a decade studying the effect of chemicals on limb development. Another expert received her doctorate in statistics from the University of California at Berkeley, and was employed as the chief of the section of the California Department of Health and Services that determines causes of birth defects. The remaining six experts had similarly impressive credentials. Contrary to the conclusion of the defendant's expert, these experts concluded that Bendectin can cause birth defects based upon: 1) test tube and live animal studies that found a link between the drug and malformations; 2) pharmacological studies examining the chemical structure of Bendectin that found similarities between the drug's structure and that of other substances known to cause birth defects; and 3) reanalysis of the previously published human statistical ("epidemiological") studies.

The District Court granted the defendant's motion for a summary judgment, stating that expert opinion based on a scientific technique is inadmissible unless the technique is "sufficiently established to have general acceptance in the field to which it belongs." The Court ruled that the plaintiffs' evidence did not meet this standard, in part because there exists such a vast body of epidemiological data concerning Bendectin that any expert opinion that is not based on epidemiological evidence is not admissible to establish causation. Thus, the test tube, live animal, and chemical structure studies performed by the plaintiffs' experts were insufficient to raise a reasonably disputable jury issue about causation. In addition, the plaintiffs' reanalyses of epidemiological studies were also ruled to be inadmissible for lack of publication and peer review.

The U.S. Court of Appeals affirmed this decision, citing *Frye v. United States* (1923). In this case, the court stated that unless expert opinion is based on a scientific technique that is "generally accepted" as reliable in the relevant scientific community, the expert's testimony is inadmissible. Because the plaintiffs' experts were basing their opinions on methodologies that diverge "significantly from the procedures accepted by recognized authorities in the field" the court declared that the techniques upon which the experts were basing their opinions "...cannot be shown to be 'generally accepted as a reliable technique.'" The unpublished reanalyses of epidemiological studies were considered by the appellate court to be especially problematic because they had not undergone the normal peer review process by others in the scientific community and had been generated solely for use in litigation. On the other hand, the original published studies that supported the defendant's position had been published and therefore had undergone full and intense scrutiny from the scientific community. Because the court ruled the plaintiffs' experts' testimony was inadmissible, it found that the plaintiffs could not meet their burden of proving causation at trial and upheld the trial court's grant of summary judgment in favor of Dow. Thus, the case was not allowed to proceed to trial.

The plaintiffs appealed to the U.S. Supreme Court. This court noted that the "general acceptance" test from *Frye* had been the dominant standard for determining the admissibility of new scientific evidence for the prior 70 years.[2] The court acknowledged that the merits of the *Frye* standard have been greatly debated, even resulting in the coining of the term "Fryologist" to describe those who take part in debates about the *Frye* case. The plaintiffs' primary argument before the court was that *Frye* was superceded by the adoption of the Federal Rules of Evidence, and as such, was not the appropriate standard to apply in their case. The Supreme Court agreed.[3]

---

[2] In *Frye*, a decision was rendered concerning the admissibility of evidence derived from a systolic blood pressure deception test, an early but crude version of the polygraph machine. The court ruled that the test had not yet gained general acceptance in the particular field in which it belongs, and ruled the evidence derived from the test to be inadmissible.

[3] It is important to note that not all state courts have adopted the Federal Rules of Evidence (Albrecht et al., 2000). In addition, the *Frye* standard still applies in some state courts. Consequently, expert witnesses should discuss the applicable state laws with the attorneys who retained them in the early stages of litigation.

Rule 402 of the Federal Rules of Evidence states that "All relevant evidence is admissible except as provided by the Constitution of the United States, by Act of Congress, by these rules, or by other rules prescribed by the Supreme Court...Evidence which is not relevant is not admissible."[4] Rule 702 specifically addresses expert testimony. At the time of the *Daubert* case, this rule stated, "If scientific, technical, or other specialized knowledge will assist the trier of fact to understand the evidence or to determine a fact in issue, a witness qualified as an expert by knowledge, skill, experience, training, or education, may testify thereto in the form of an opinion or otherwise." Note that "general acceptance" is not included in this rule as a requirement for admissibility.

Rule 702 specifies that an expert's testimony can meet the standard established by this rule if two tests are met. First, the testimony must be related to an area outside the understanding of the average lay person (e.g., scientific, technical, or other specialized knowledge). And second, the witness must qualify as an expert in the particular subject area. This second test will be met if the witness has knowledge, skill, experience, training, or education in the subject area that makes the witness an expert.

The Court mandated that trial judges make a pretrial determination of whether expert scientific testimony should be admitted:

> "Faced with a proffer of expert scientific testimony, then, the trial judge must determine at the outset whether the expert is proposing to testify to (1) scientific knowledge that (2) will assist the trier of fact to understand or determine a fact in issue. This entails a preliminary assessment of whether the reasoning or methodology underlying the testimony is scientifically valid and of whether that reasoning or methodology properly can be applied to the facts in issue. Many factors will bear on this inquiry, and we do not presume to set out a definitive checklist or test..."

---

[4] Rule 401 defines "relevant evidence" quite broadly, as that which has "any tendency to make the existence of any fact that is of consequence to the determination of the action more probable or less probable than it would be without the evidence."

Thus, the trial judge has a "gatekeeping role" to screen the supposedly scientific evidence and to ensure that the evidence is relevant and reliable before it is admitted.

While the Court did not attempt to develop a definitive checklist or test for the trial judge to employ when making the determination of the admissibility of scientific (or technical or specialized knowledge) testimony, it provided four factors that a judge might employ when making this decision:

1) can the theory or technique be tested;

2) has the theory or technique been subjected to peer review and publication;

3) what is the technique's known or potential rate of error; or

4) is the theory or technique generally accepted within its scientific community.

The Ninth Circuit Court, upon appeal, added a fifth factor – did the theory or technique exist prior to the litigation.

Finally, the Supreme Court addressed the defendant's expressed apprehension at abandoning the "general acceptance" requirement for admissibility. The Court did not agree with the defendant's position that a "…'free for all' in which befuddled juries are confounded by absurd and irrational pseudoscientific assertions" would result. On the contrary, the Court expressed its opinion that the traditional methods of attacking shaky but admissible evidence – vigorous cross examination, presentation of contrary evidence, and careful instruction on the burden of proof – would continue to serve the adversarial system well.

Does *Daubert* apply to nonscientific experts?

One of the greatest areas of controversy since the issuance of the Court's opinion in *Daubert* is whether the ruling also applies to nonscientific experts. This controversy was settled by the U.S. Supreme Court in *Kumho Tire Company, Ltd. v. Patrick Carmichael* in March 1999, when the Court issued the opinion that *Daubert* does apply to the testimony of engineers and other experts who are not scientists.[5]

---

[5] Kumho was involved an incident where the right rear tire of a minivan separated and blew out. In the ensuing accident, one passenger died and others were badly injured. Plaintiffs sued Kumho Tire, claiming that the tire was defective. The plaintiffs predicated the case significantly upon proffered expert testimony to which the defendants objected.

Specifically, the Court ruled that:

1) the *Daubert* gatekeeping role of determining that expert testimony is relevant and reliable — and therefore admissible — applies to all expert testimony, not only "scientific" testimony. Rule 702 of the Federal Rules of Evidence does not distinguish between scientific, technical, or other specialized knowledge. The Court's language in its *Daubert* decision focused on scientific evidence because that was the nature of the case. The "...objective is to make certain that an expert employs in the courtroom the same level of intellectual rigor that characterized the practice of an expert in the relevant field;"

2) when determining the admissibility of expert testimony, the responsibility of the trial judge is to determine "...whether the testimony has a 'reliable basis' in the knowledge and experience of [the relevant discipline]." Thus, a trial judge may consider any of the four specific *Daubert* factors when it is sensible to apply them to the facts of the case at hand, together with any other factors that the trial judge finds useful; and

3) if an expert applies a theory that is generally accepted by the relevant scientific community, it must have been properly applied with respect to the particular case.

In response to *Daubert* and *Kumho*, Rule 702 of the Federal Rules of Evidence was modified to specifically include the standards established by the Supreme Court in those cases. Rule 702 now reads: "If scientific, technical, or other specialized knowledge will assist the trier of fact to understand the evidence or to determine a fact in issue, a witness qualified as an expert by knowledge, skill, experience, training, or education, may testify thereto in the form of an opinion or otherwise, if (1) the testimony is based upon sufficient facts or data, (2) the testimony is the product of reliable principles and methods, and (3) the witness has applied the principles and methods reliably to the facts of the case." The revised Rule allows trial courts to exercise considerable discretion when developing reasonable measures of reliability in a particular case. Note that the factors used by a trial judge to determine admissibility of expert testimony depend upon the particular discipline that is relevant to the issue, and the focus is upon the expert's means of analysis, not the expert's conclusions.

Thus, accountants hired to testify as expert witnesses are held to the standards established by the Supreme Court in *Daubert* since accountants would be considered nonscientific experts. In fact, the *Daubert* decision has been applied to accountants in many cases (see Exhibit 1).

EXHIBIT 1
Examples of Recent Cases in Which *Daubert* Has Been Applied to Accountants

A. A. Profiles, Inc. v. City of Fort Lauderdale, 253 F.3d 576 (11th Cir. 2001)

Biben v. Card, et al., 1994 WL 705258 (W.D. Mo.)

Bragdon v. Davenport, No 99-1643 (1st Cir. 2000)

Children's Broadcasting Corp. v. The Walt Disney Co., 245 F.3d 1008 (8th Cir. 2001)

City of Tuscaloosa v. Harcros Chemicals, Inc. 158 F.3d 548 (11th Cir. 1998)

Creative Dimensions in Management, Inc. v. Thomas Group, Inc., 1999 WL 225890 (E.D. Pa)

David Otis v. Doctor's Associates, Inc., et al., 1998 WL 673595 (N.D. Ill.)

De Jager Const. Inc. v. Schleininger, 938 F. Supp. 446 (W.D. Mich. 1996)

Drago v. Aetna Plywood, Inc., 1998 WL 474100 (N.D. Ill.)

Ed Peters Jewelry Co., Inc. v. C & J Jewelry Co., Inc. et al., 124 F.3d 252 (1st Cir. 1997)

Forklifts of St. Louis, Inc. v. Komatsu Forklift, USA, Inc., 178 F.3d 1030 (8th Cir. 1998)

Frymire-Brinati v. KPMG Peat Marwick, 2 F.3d 183 (7th Cir. 1993)

GT Laboratories, Inc. v. The Cooper Companies, Inc., 1998 WL 704302 (N.D. Ill.)

Israel Travel Advisory Service, Inc. v. Israel Identity Tours, Inc., 1993 WL 387346 (N.D. Ill.)

JMJ Enterprises, Inc. v. Via Veneto Italian Ice, Inc., 1998 WL 175888 (E.D.Pa.)

William I. Koch v. Koch Industries, Inc., 2 F. Supp. 2d 1385 (D. Kan. 1998)

Lieberman v. The American Dietetic Association, 1996 WL 521176 (N.D. Ill. No. 94 C4227)

Lithuanian Commerce Corp. v. Sara Lee Hosiery, 179 F.R.D. 450 (D.N.J. 1998)

Masayesva v. Hale, 118 F.3d 1371 (9th Cir. 1997)

Morse/Diesel, Inc. v. Trinity Industries, Inc., 67 F.3d 435 (2nd Cir. 1995)

Nilssen v. Motorola, Inc., 1998 WL 513090 (N.D. Ill.)

Ohio v. Louis Trauth Dairy, Inc., 925 F. Supp. 1247 (S.D. Ohio 1996)

Parkway Garage, Inc. v. City of Philadelphia, et al., 1994 WL 412430 (E.D. Pa.)

Pfizer Inc. v. Advanced Monobloc, Corp., 1999 WL 743927 (Del. Super.)

Robert Billet Promotions, Inc. v. IMI Cornelius, Inc., 1998 WL 721081 (E.D. Pa.)

Robertson v. Commissioner of Internal Revenue, No. 99-71368 (9th Cir. 2001)

Sanchez v. KPMG Peat Marwick, 1996 U.S. Dist. LEXIS 2773 (D.N.M.)

SEC v. Lipson, 46 F. Supp. 2d 758 (N.D. Ill. No. 97 C2661 1999)

Target Marketing Pub. Inc. v. ADVO, Inc., 136 F.3d 1139 (7th Cir. 1998)

Taylor v. United States, 1994 WL 421485 (M.D. Ala.)

Three Crown Ltd. Partnership v. Salomon Bros., Inc., 906 F. Supp. 876 (S.D. N.Y 1995)

TRW Title Insurance Company v. Security Union Title Insurance Company, 890 F. Supp. 756 (N.D. Ill. 1995)

Tuf Racing Products, Inc. v. American Suzuki Motor Corp., 223 F.3d 585 (7th Cir. 2000)

Turck v. Baker Petrolite Corp., No. 00-5082 (10th Cir. 2000)

United Phosporus Ltd. v. Midland Fumigant, Inc., 173 F.R.D. 675 (D. Kan. 1997)

United States v. Glennahee, No. 99-1991 (6th Cir. 2001)

United States v. Sparks, No. 99-6387 (10th Cir. 2001)

United States v. Tarwater, 308 F.3d 494 (6th Cir. 2002)

Value Co. v. US Air, Inc., 979 F. Supp. 731 (M.D. Ill. 1997)

Vaulting & Cash Services, Inc. v. Diebold Incorporated, 1998 WL 726070 (E.D. La.)

ADMISSIBILITY OF THE EXPERT'S TESTIMONY

Before ruling whether the expert's testimony is admissible, the trial judge must make two determinations: 1) is the person qualified to serve as an expert witness? and 2) will the testimony of the expert aid the jury in understanding the evidence or determining a fact at issue? This second determination is where the *Daubert* case has an effect because the court must satisfy its gatekeeper role of ensuring that the conclusions reached by the expert are based on scientific principles or some generally accepted test of reliability.

Is the Person Qualified to Serve as an Expert Witness?

An individual is qualified to serve as an expert witness if the person possesses special knowledge, skill, experience, training, or education regarding the subject matter of the testimony (e.g., fraud investigations). Credentials such as licensing or certification, published books or journal articles, or positions in professional associations or organizations can also be offered as evidence of being qualified to testify as an expert.

Before being allowed to testify as an expert, the individual's qualifications must be stated. Sometimes the expert's resume (curriculum vitae) will be submitted as an exhibit. In some cases, the opposing attorney may agree to stipulate that the individual is qualified. Even if this occurs, the attorney for whom the witness is testifying may wish to state the expert's main credentials so the judge and jury will hear them in an attempt to increase the credibility of the expert.

Usually, the witness's qualifications are not contested. More often, opposing counsel will seek to disqualify an expert from testifying by making a challenge under *Daubert*.

Challenges under *Daubert*

The second determination the trial judge must make in order to rule whether an expert's testimony is admissible is whether the testimony of the expert will aid the jury in understanding the evidence or determining a fact at issue. This determination is where the *Daubert* case has an effect because the court must meet its gatekeeping role and ensure that the expert's conclusions are based on evidence that is relevant and reliable. Opposing counsel will often seek to exclude the expert's testimony on the basis that the *Daubert* standards for admissibility are not met. Hence, the term "*Daubert* challenge" was born.

More specifically, a "*Daubert* challenge" is a motion in limine made by legal counsel to prevent an opposing expert witness from testifying on the grounds that the expert's testimony is based on faulty, unreliable data.[6] Generally, the motion is made after the deadline for naming expert, and thus, if the motion is granted it can severely damage the opposing party's case.

Grummons v. Bridgestone/Firestone, Inc.

In a recent case in Federal District Court in Montana (*Grummons v. Bridgestone/Firestone, Inc.*), a nonscientific expert was ruled qualified to testify as an expert in an alleged defective tire case despite opposing counsel's efforts to raise a *Daubert* challenge against the expert. Since any auditor, accountant, or CPA serving as an expert witness would fall into the category of a "nonscientific" expert, this court case can provide some guidance in how to successfully meet such challenges.

In *Grummons v. Bridgestone/Firestone, Inc.*, the nature of the plaintiffs' case was that a tire of the defendant's caused a dangerous driving condition called "oversteer." This condition made the car directionally unstable and resulted in a one car rollover accident. The plaintiffs alleged that the tires were driven according to the defendant's recommendations. Despite driving per the manufacturer's recommendations, the tires wore unevenly, thus producing the oversteer. Further, the defendant failed to warn or advise the plaintiffs how expected wear would change a vehicle's handling characteristics. The plaintiffs relied upon an investigation of the tires in question by a person they intended to proffer as an expert. The defendant moved to exclude him under *Daubert* and *Kumho*, making challenges pertaining to the expert's qualifications and methodology.

The defendant challenged the expert for lack of education and experience with tire design or manufacture. The essence of the defendant's motion

---

[6] A motion in limine is a request before the trial that evidence of the opposing side be ruled to be inadmissible.

was that the expert had no education or experience that qualified him to render opinions about how the tires factored into causing the accident. The expert had a bachelor of science degree in mechanical engineering. While the plaintiffs' expert had not been employed in the automotive or tire industry, he designed devices to test the tires, in addition to field testing tires of the same type.

The trial court described the defendant's argument as "wholly without merit." How this expert convinced the trial court of his qualifications can be a lesson for other nonscientific experts.

The court considered the following facts about the expert witness:

1) He was a registered mechanical engineer with several years of teaching experience in the engineering college of a state university;

2) He was employed as a consulting engineer. In this capacity he had designed and built instruments for the automobile industry to measure power output in order to help analyze appropriate chassis configuration;

3) He had driven upon tires of the type in question as a consumer for six years and as an autocross-racing competitor for five years;

4) He read at least 19 technical documents from the Society of Automotive Engineers that pertained to theories about the subjects at issue and included literature about how to conduct scientific investigation of the handling characteristics of tires;

5) He devised experiments to test the theories in reliance upon his engineering training, experience, and reference to the technical manuals. This process was the same process of innovation the expert used in designing and testing machinery for his consulting business. The self-designed devices were susceptible to objective testing in order to measure their reliability. As such, they were not designed to reach a predetermined result; and

6) He relied on deposition testimony from other experts in the case as sources for the data incorporated into his opinion. The reliability and relevance of the data was unquestionable.

The court implicitly recognized that the market value of the expert's skills and methodology added credibility to his approach of testing the product in question. The application of market tested methodologies to data and facts not in dispute helped convince the court that the expert was qualified under the *Daubert* and *Kumho* standards of relevance and reliability.

IMPLICATIONS FOR ACCOUNTANTS AS EXPERT WITNESSES

The implications of *Daubert* and *Kumho* to a testifying accountant in a dispute are significant. For example, one can expect that accountants frequently will be asked to "assist the trier of fact" due to the concealment feature that inevitably is present in fraud. Accountants can provide unique assistance to the jury in testifying how the fraud occurred and providing an estimate of the magnitude of the fraud. These facts are not always easy to determine, given that often the fraud perpetrator was a long-time, trusted employee who had a large degree of control over the accounting information system. Documents needed to conclusively prove the extent of the fraud might have been destroyed by the perpetrator prior to the discovery of the fraud. Similarly, one can expect accountants to be asked to serve as expert witnesses in other forensic accounting cases, such as divorce or bankruptcy proceedings.

Accountants should expect that opposing counsel will challenge their credentials and expertise at every opportunity. No one can pretend to predict with certainty what a trial court will rule. Accountants nevertheless should face *Daubert* challenges with confidence, even if they are inexperienced as forensic investigators. A practicing accountant is in much the same situation as the *Grummons* expert, in that successful practice shows expertise. The accountant can also show expertise in ways that are usual to the profession. Attending conferences and seminars, reading professional literature, writing and publishing articles, participating in developing standards recognized by professional organizations, possessing professional certification, and consulting with other professionals indicate currency and capability.

Of greater importance is the expert's use of accepted methodology of the profession (Summerford, 2002; Kozinski, 2001). Judges are not accountants. They will not challenge the standards or procedures of the accounting profession. Their concern is simply whether the expert's accounting knowledge is relevant and reliable. Basically, the question the judge is asking is "Does the accountant know what he or she is talking about?" The answer is yes if the accountant worked as other professional accountants would in the same circumstances.

So how might an accountant fail a *Daubert* challenge and be disqualified as an expert witness? A review of several recent federal court holdings on the admittance of accountants as experts reveals that accountants are disqualified when they grossly depart from the standards of the profession.

For example, in *Target Marketing Pub, Inc. v. ADVO, Inc.* (1998), the accountant failed to incorporate into his opinion, without explanation, some of his own findings that contradicted his testimony. This situation also occurred in the *Kumbo* case discussed earlier, and that engineering expert's testimony was also excluded under *Daubert*. The appearance is that the expert manufactured his opinion to embellish the case of the party that engaged him. In *SEC v. Lipson* (1998), the accountant testified from unaudited financial reports, did not analyze data covering the entire period of time in question, did not compare revenue to budget projections of revenue, and "...[allowed his] opinion about the objective reality of certain records to be influenced by the subjective statements of an interested party...". Similarly, in *Lithuania Commerce Corp. v. Sara Lee Hosiery* (1998), the expert's testimony was excluded by the trial court because the expert, in comparing hosiery made by different manufacturers, relied upon an inadequate sample and destroyed the records of his methodology.

In contrast, consider *Forklifts of St. Louis, Inc. v. Komatsu Forklift, USA, Inc.* (1998). The CPA's testimony about the plaintiff's damages was allowed where he relied upon the books, records, and financial reports of the plaintiff. The court stated that the motion not to admit the testimony of the accountant was "absurd." The defendant's attorney vigorously cross-examined the expert, and the jury reduced the award from what the accountant recommended by one-third. However, the CPA's expertise and methodology survived the *Daubert* challenge made by opposing counsel, and he was allowed to testify. The fact that the CPA was vigorously cross-examined by opposing counsel is exactly what is to be expected when an expert survives a *Daubert* challenge. Recall that the U.S. Supreme Court expressed its opinion in the *Daubert* case that the traditional methods of attacking shaky but admissible evidence – vigorous cross examination, presentation of contrary evidence, and careful instruction on the burden of proof – would continue to serve the adversarial system well.

Similarly, in *City of Tuscaloosa v. Harcros Chemicals, Inc.* (1998), the accountant testified about damages connected to price fixing and fraud. He calculated, compiled and explained costs incurred and revenues generated by chemical distributors. He studied the defendant's costs of material, labor, overhead, transportation, depreciation, insurance, and other expenses. The appellate court ruled that the trial court properly admitted the testimony of the expert that was derived from the records of the defendant.

In applying *Daubert* and *Kumho*, courts are sensitive to the theories, knowledge and methodologies of professions. This flexible approach accommodates professional advances. Experts who follow the standards and methods of their professions and document their efforts generally will pass over the *Daubert* bar.

SUMMARY

A review of available fraud statistics suggests that the demand for auditors and forensic accountants to testify in court will continue to grow (e.g., see ACFE, 2002; Ernst & Young, 2000; KPMG, 1998). *Daubert* impresses upon counsel the need for competent experts. The flexible approach adopted by the courts of determining whether an expert's testimony is relevant and reliable is respectful of individual professions. As such, it contemplates that the accounting profession itself will define its members' credentials, methodology, theory, and specialized knowledge.

Attorneys will be aggressive in searching for the best-qualified experts to testify for their cases because juries rely heavily on expert testimony. Consequently, lawyers will vigorously attack the credentials and methodologies of opposing experts while jealously protecting and promoting their own experts from similar attacks. Accountants who have knowledge and skill that is customary in the profession and who demonstrate that they have applied that knowledge and skill to the particular issues of a case will survive a *Daubert* challenge. Conversely, experts who use unsupported assertions in their testimony or otherwise do not adhere to the standards of the accounting profession will not be allowed to testify.

REFERENCES

Albrecht, W. S., D. R. Carmichael, M. M. Stanton, D. K. Wilson, M. L. Reed, and C. W. Shipp. (2000). *Guide to Fraud Investigations*, Fourth Edition. Practitioners Publishing Company: Fort Worth, Texas.

The Association of Certified Fraud Examiners. (2002). *2002 Report to the Nation Occupational Fraud and Abuse.* Austin, TX: ACFE.

City of Tuscaloosa v. Harcros Chemicals, Inc. 158 F.3d 548 (11th Cir. 1998).

Daubert v. Merrell Dow Pharmaceutical, 509 U.S. 579 (1993).

Ernst & Young. (2000). *Fraud: The Unmanaged Risk. An International Survey of the Effects of Fraud on Business.* London, UK: Ernst & Young.

Forklifts of St. Louis, Inc. v. Komatsu Forklift, USA, Inc., 178 F.3d 1030 (8th Cir. 1998).

Frye v. United States, 54 App. D.C. 46, 293 F. 1013 (1923).

Grummons v. Bridgestone/Firestone, Inc., CV 99-043-BU-RWA (2001).

Kozinski, A. (2001). Expert Testimony After *Daubert... Journal of Accountancy* (July): 59 – 62.

KPMG Peat Marwick. (1998). 1998 *Fraud Survey*. Montvale, NJ: KPMG Peat Marwick.

Kumho Tire Company, Ltd. v. Patrick Carmichael, 526 U.S. 137, 119 S.Ct. 1167 (1999).

Lithuanian Commerce Corp. v. Sara Lee Hosiery, 179 F.R.D. 450 (D.N.J. 1998).

SEC v. Lipson, 46 F.Supp.2d 758 (N.D.Ill. 1998).

Summerford, R. (2002). Expert Witnessing: The Changing Landscape. *The White Paper: Topical Issues on White-Collar Crime* (July/August): 34 – 37, 51 – 53.

Target Marketing Pub, Inc. v. ADVO, Inc., 136 F.3d 1139 (7th Cir. 1998).

Wells, J. T., N. S. Bradford, G. Geis, J. D. Gill, W. M. Kramer, J. D. Ratley, and J. C. Robertson. (1998). *Fraud Examiners Manual*, Third Edition, Updated 2000-2001. Association of Certified Fraud Examiners: Austin, Texas.

CHAPTER 5

Qualifying as an Expert Witness

D. Larry Crumbley

There are many ways for expert witness to be excluded from the court-room. Both simple and complex *Daubert* and *Frye* challenges are becoming frequent as tort costs climb. Accountants must take the qualification process seriously in order to avoid adversely affecting clients and their personal reputation. Lack of independence, conflicts of interest, side-taking, and result-oriented work are situations to avoid.

Forensic accounting can be broken into two broad categories: investigative accounting and litigation services. Under either category an accountant may be required to testify in the courtroom. Forensic accountants work with attorneys, private investigators, law enforcement officers, corporate security specialists, the IRS, and the FBI. An excerpt from a novel provides a description of an expert testifying in the courtroom:[1]

> "Briefly forensic accounting is a science that deals with the relation and application of facts to business and social problems." Lenny smiled and turned towards the jury. "As I tell my students, a forensic accountant is like the Columbo or Quincy character of yesteryears, except he or she uses accounting records and facts to uncover fraud, missing assets, insider tradings, and other white collar crimes." Lenny turned back to the pinstriped lawyer.

How an individual can qualify as an expert witness varies depending on whether the litigation is in federal or state courts. The federal courts and

[1] I.W. Collett & M. Smith, *Trap Doors and Trojan Horses*, Thomas Horton & Daughters p. 76

Dr. Crumbley is the KPMG Endowed Professor at Louisiana State University. Portions of this article have been adapted from his book *Forensic and Investigative Accounting*, published by Commerce Clearing House.

many states have adopted the *Daubert* standard. Some states follow the older *Frye* standard, and other states have their own standard (e.g., North Carolina balances relevancy or materiality against prejudicial effect).[2]

There are two different courtroom environments: civil and criminal. Some experts believe it is more difficult to convict in a criminal trial. E.J. McMillan says "you have to remember one thing, and this is the fact that our laws aren't designed to punish guilty people; they're intended to protect innocent people."[3] And Clinton McKinzie says "I have never come to terms with a system based on the principal that it is better to let hundreds of guilty people go free rather than wrongly convict one innocent person. It's okay for people to be victimized again and again as long as no one is mistakenly locked up."[4] In a civil trial, however, the jurors try to give away as much money as possible, because it is not their money, and there are no guilt feelings.

U.S. TORT COSTS CLIMBING

The U.S. tort system cost $246 billion in 2003, which is $845 per U.S. citizen ($12 in 1950). U.S. tort costs accounted for 2.23% of GDP (similar to 2002). Increasingly inefficient, the U.S. tort system returns less than 50 cents on the dollar to people it is designed to help; only about 22 cents to compensate for actual loss. Medical malpractice costs totaled nearly $27 billion in 2003, or $91 per person (compared to $5 per person in 1975). Tort costs increased by a total of 33.5% in the past three years.[5] Some of these costs are expert witnessing fees.

THE DISPUTE BEGINS

John Grisham gives two major ways to sue in the civil courts: 1) by ambush, or 2) serve and volley. With an ambush, the attorney prepares a

---

[2] The following internet sites keep track of the states that still follow *Frye*. http://faculty.ncwc.edu/toconnor/daubert.htm, and http://www.effingham.net/michael/dbtp.html.

[3] E.J. McMillan, *The Audit, MD*: Harwood Publishing, 2000, p. 259.

[4] Clinton Mckinzie, *The Edge of Justice*, New York: Bantam Dell, 2002.

[5] Tillinghast-Tower Perrin, *U.S. Tort Costs: 2004 Update*, December 10, 2004.

skeletal framework of the allegations, runs to the courthouse, files the suit, leaks it to the press, and hopes he or she can prove what is alleged. A serve and volley begins with a letter to the defendants, making the same allegations, but rather than suing, the attorney invites a discussion. Letters go back and forth trying to reach a compromise so litigation can be avoided.[6] The five major phases of litigation are

- Pleadings
- Discovery
- Trial
- Outcome
- Possible appeal

Much of the work for forensic accountants occur in the discovery stage.

The pleadings consist of

- **Complaint** – Plaintiff files.
- **Service of Process** – served on defendant.
- **Answer** – Defendant must admit or deny allegations.
- **Demurrer**- No cause of action exists.
- **Possible cross-complaint**

An attorney's job is to ultimately avoid trial and the resulting lost time and expenses. Thus, the goal of a forensic accountant is to help the attorney to avoid the cost and uncertainty of a trial.[7]

One has the right to a jury trial in district courts, but jurors can only determine the facts and not the law. There is no jury trial in probate, family law, estate issues, equitable issue, U.S. Tax Court, and U.S. Court of Federal Claims. There is an automatic right to appeal from trial courts to the first level of the appellate process. But higher courts (e.g., Supreme Court) must decide whether to hear the dispute. In order to get to federal courts, one must raise the question of a federal law or diversity of citizenship (e.g., different state). For the federal court, the controversy must exceed $50,000. State courts have trial courts, appeal courts, and a supreme court.

---

[6] John Grisham, *The Street Lawyer*, New York: Bantam Dell, 1998, p. 274.

[7] H. Silverstone and M. Sheetz, *Forensic Accounting and Fraud Investigation*, Hoboken, N.J.: John Wiley & Sons, 2004, p. 233,

During the trial the attorneys each act in the role of opposing movie director's – calling witnesses and orchestrating carefully timed presentations.
All of it is designed to sway the jury's disposition in favor of their respective client's position. Civil cases are decided based only on which side has
the greatest preponderance of evidence in its favor. Evidence of guilt or
innocence beyond a reasonable doubt is the criterion for deciding criminal cases only, and therefore do not apply to civil cases.[8]

There are number of ways for the other side to attempt to challenge an
expert:

1. *Daubert* challenges.

2. *Frye* challenges.

3. Does not qualify as an expert by knowledge, skill, experience,
    training, or education.

4. Requires a valid connection to the pertinent inquiry as a precon-
    dition to admission.

5. Courts remain vigilant against the admission of legal conclusions.

6. In *re Paoli Railroad Yard PCB Litigation*, 35 F.3d 717 (3rd Cir.
    1994) lists others.

    a. Relationships of technique to methods already established to
        be reliable.

    b. Existence and maintenance of standards controlling tech-
        nique's operation.

    c. Expert witness' qualifications and non-judicial uses to which
        method has been put.

7. Side-taking or result – oriented work.

8. Conflict of interest.

---

[8] I.W. Collett and D. Forgione, *Costly Reflections in a Midas Mirror*, Thomas Horton and
Daughters, 1995, p. 131

9. Ghost-written report.

10. Spoliation.

11. Name not disclosed within time limit.

12. Improper expert witness designation.

FRYE STANDARD

Before *Daubert* was decided, the dominant standard for determining the admissibility of expert testimony was the *Frye* standard. Under the *Frye* standard, which no longer is used in federal courts but still is used by many state courts (at least 14), the test for admitting expert testimony is (1) whether the expert's testimony will assist the trier of fact in understanding the evidence or in determining a fact in issue and (2) whether the theories and/or techniques relied upon by the expert are generally accepted by the relevant professional community, and (3) whether the particular expert is qualified to present expert testimony on the subject at issue.[9]

Judges applying the *Frye* standard review what an expert's peers have written and said about the expert's theories and/or techniques to determine whether those theories and/or techniques have gained general acceptance in the relevant professional community. Judges applying the *Frye* standard defer to an expert's peers to determine whether the expert's testimony should be admitted into evidence. By contrast, under the *Daubert* standard, judges themselves are required to assess the reliability of an expert's theories and/or techniques.

DAUBERT STANDARD

In *Daubert v. Merrell Dow Pharmaceuticals, Inc.*,[10] the United States Supreme Court established the rule for federal courts that trial judges have a special responsibility to ensure that scientific testimony is not only relevant, but also reliable. In *Kumho Tire Company, Ltd. v. Carmichael*,[11] the

[9] Frye v. U.S., 293 F. 1013 (DC Cir. 1923).
[10] 509 U.S. 579, 113 S.Ct 2786 (1993).
[11] 526 U.S. 137, 119 S.Ct 1167 (1999).

Supreme Court decided that a judge's "gatekeeping" obligation applies not only to scientific testimony but to all expert testimony. The *Daubert* case and its progeny have had a substantial impact on forensic accounting methods and reasoning in general. These decisions have resulted in heightened scrutiny in many instances of not only the methods used but the underlying factual support for the conclusions presented.

Under the Federal Rules of Evidence, a judge will permit an accountant to testify as an expert witness only if the judge decides that:

> The accountant's testimony will help the jurors or judge understand the evidence or determine a fact in issue.[12]

> The accountant is qualified as an expert by knowledge, skill, experience, training, or education.[13]

> The accountant can show that his or her testimony (a) will be based on sufficient facts or data and (b) will be the product of reliable principles and methods that have been applied reliably to the facts of the dispute.[14]

Before permitting an individual to testify as an expert, a judge will determine whether the expert's reasoning and methodology can appropriately be applied to the facts of the dispute.[15] Also, the judge must take into consideration the expert's background and practical experience when deciding whether an expert is qualified to render an opinion.[16] A judge may decide that an expert is insufficiently qualified because his or her expertise is too general or too deficient.[17] A judge also may decide that studies cited are too dissimilar to the facts involved in the litigation.[18]

---

[12] Rule 702 of the Federal Rules of Evidence.

[13] Rule 702 of the Federal Rules of Evidence.

[14] Rule 702 of the Federal Rules of Evidence.

[15] *Stagl v. Delta Airlines, Inc.*, 117 F.3d 81 (CA-2, 1997).

[16] *McColluck v. H.B. Fuller Co.*, 61 F.3d 1043 (CA-2 1995).

[17] *Trumps v. Toastmaster*, 969 F. Supp. 252 (S.D. N.Y. 1997).

[18] *General Electric Co. v. Joiner*, 522 US 136, 118 S.Ct. 512 (1997).

There may be simple *Daubert* challenges or complex *Daubert* challenges. A simple *Daubert* challenge involves a motion of limine and a motion of summary judgment. Once documents are filed, there is a hearing with the judge and lawyers. The motion for summary judgment may or may not be granted.

A complex *Daubert* challenge may involve multiple-day hearings. There can be live witnesses with challenged experts and rebuttal experts.

DAUBERT FACTORS

Various factors are considered to determine whether an expert's testimony rests on a reliable foundation and properly can be applied to the facts at issue. In *Daubert*,[19] the United States Supreme Court suggested that judges consider the following factors:

Whether the theory or technique in question can be (and has been) tested.

Whether the theory or technique in question has been subjected to peer review and publication.

The theory's or techniques' known or potential error rate.

Whether the theory or technique has attracted widespread acceptance within the relevant community.

The Ninth Circuit Court of Appeals[20] added another consideration: *Whether the theory or technique existed before litigation began.* Daubert decisions are made at the trial court level. The U.S. Supreme Court has held that the abuse-of-discretion standard ordinarily applied to review evidentiary rulings is the proper standard by which to review a trial court's decision to admit or exclude expert testimony.[21]

---

[19] 509 U.S. 579, 113 SCt 2786 (1993).

[20] *Daubert v. Merrell Dow Pharmaceuticals, Inc.*, 43 F.3d 1311(CA-9, 1995).

[21] *General Electric Company v. Joiner*, 522 U.S. 136, 118 S.Ct 512 (1997).

Litigants increasingly have been making successful *Daubert* challenges. One searchable database of *Daubert* and *Kumho Tire* decisions, the *Daubert Tracker*, had 93 accounting decisions in mid-February 2003.[22] Of the 93 accounting expert cases, 46 percent of the experts were admitted, 38 percent were denied admission, and 9 percent were admitted/denied in part. Another online service tracking *Daubert* cases, *Daubert on the Web*,[23] in mid January 2005 listed 67 cases under the field "Accountants and Economists" and an admissibility rate of .627. This rate compares with .828 for criminologists, .400 for marketing experts, .138 for polygraphers, .333 for toxicologists, and .667 for computer experts.

Just saying that one is a CPA (or some other professional designation) will not automatically qualify an accountant as an expert. CPAs who wish to testify as an expert witness have to convince a judge that they should be considered an expert about the matter being litigated and that their testimony will be relevant and reliable. A CPA must carefully set out what the AICPA professional standards are, explain what CPA certification requires, and why he or she is entitled to be an expert in a particular situation. The accountant must put this CPA evidence in every case so that on appeal the information is in the record.[24] If a trial judge says that the testimony of an expert is admissible, there is almost no way that the decision to admit evidence will be reversed on appeal.[25] But this is not a hard-and-fast rule.

In a franchise termination suit, the Seventh Circuit said that a CPA was not doing science, he was doing accounting. Based on financial information furnished by plaintiff and assumptions supplied by counsel, he calculated discounted present value of lost future earnings. Accountants are qualified to do that.[26]

---

[22] www.mdexonline.com. A year subscription is $495.

[23] www.daubertontheweb.com.

[24] 8 Alex Kozinski, "Expert Testimony After Daubert," *Journal of Accountancy* (July 2001), pp. 59-60.

[25] Alex Kozinski, "Expert Testimony After Daubert," *Journal of Accountancy* (July 2001), p. 60; V.J. Love and D.L. Goldwasser, "Update on the Preclusion of Financial Experts Under Daubert," *The CPA Journal* (July 1999); *Irvine v. Murad Skin Research Lab.*, 194 F.3d 313 (CA 1 1999).

For example, a CPA's testimony about an insider trading defendant was inadmissible because the methodology used for the CPA's opinion was no more than speculation.[27] An accounting expert who valued property using a discounted cash flow analysis and assigned no value to raw land and a large office building was not allowed to testify.[28] An economist's testimony concerning loss figures for guidance or counsel for financial support was inadmissible because it was not based on scientifically valid methodology.[29] The testimony by a former tax prosecutor that the government should not have filed a criminal tax case was inadmissible.[30]

DAUBERT Challenges

Paschal Baute has advised experts to include the following information in their expert's affidavit to overcome *Daubert* challenges:[31]

- State that the conclusion or opinion rendered is "within reasonable degree of medical or scientific certainty."

- Specifically state the conclusion of the independent research relied upon.

- Name the scientific scrutiny and peer review to which the studies or methodologies have been subjected.

- Name the independent objective sources supporting the conclusion reached.

Accountants should take the qualification process seriously. Their disqualification can adversely affect not only their client but also their personal reputation. If their expert testimony is inadmissible, the lawsuit may be over. For example, a plaintiff lost a breach of contract and breach of fiduciary duty dispute by summary judgment because the plaintiff's accounting expert report was "pure speculation, based upon utterly implausible assumptions and unreliable methodology."[32]

---

[27] *SEC v. Lipson*, 46 F. Supp. 2d 758 (N.D. Ill. 1999).

[28] *Frymire Brinati v. KPMG Peat Marwick*, 2 F.3d 183 (CA-9, 1993).

[29] *Cochrane v. Schneider Natl. Carriers, Inc.*, 980 F. Supp. 374 (D. Kan. 1996).

[30] *U.S. v. Rice*, 52 F.3d 843 (CA-10, 1995), cert. denied, 116 S.Ct. 2536 (1996).

[31] For more information, see *Mealey's Daubert Report*, Mealey's Publications, King of Prussia, PA. P.O. Box 62090, 19406 0230.

[32] *Target Market Publishing Co. v. ADVO, Inc.*, 136 F.3d 1139 (CA-7, 1998).

If accountants claim expertise about a matter, do work for a litigant, and are rejected as expert witnesses, a litigant may bring a malpractice claim against them. Accountants who are excluded several times on *Daubert* challenges may find themselves discredited. Further, judges can hurt an expert witness' reputation by making negative comments about the expert in open courtroom. A judge in Florida's Fourth District Court of Appeal said the following about an expert when a defense attorney asked why he excluded the expert:"Dr. ____ is an insidious perjurer who would-n't know the truth if it leapt up and bit him on the ***." The expert is a doctor since 1963 and has testified for 25 years. On appeal the appellate court upheld the judge's ruling that the expert's claim lacked merit.

On January 6, 2005, Andrea Yates' capital murder conviction for drowning her children was overturned by an appeals court because of Dr. Park Dietz's erroneous testimony about a nonexistent TV episode on Law & Order. His photo was shown on Fox News, and the talking heads called him a "hired gun" and a "whore." One talking head said that "he's dead."

In an anti-trust dispute a District Court excluded an economist and award-ed summary judgment to plaintiff. The Fourth Circuit affirmed the exclu-sion, saying that the expert had an MBA and significant executive experi-ence in the relevant industry, but he subscribed to no economics journals, could identify no economics journals, had published no economics-relat-ed articles, was unfamiliar with basic terms employed by economists in anti-trust analysis, had never conducted any relevant market analysis, and had read only materials provided to him by counsel.[33]

In another dispute the Fifth Circuit said just because the expert had a MD degree was not enough to qualify him to give an opinion on every con-ceivable question.[34]

Accountants can run afoul of *Daubert* if they do not stick with generally accepted principles, they do not apply generally accepted principles con-sistently, they cannot explain how their conclusion follows from generally accepted principles, or they rely on bad information. Accountants should be skeptical of any information given to them by their client.

---

[33] *Berlyn, Inc. v. Gazette Newspapers. Inc.*, No. 02-2152 (CA-4. Aug. 18, 2003) (unpub-lished).

[34] *Christopherson v. Allied Signal Corp.*, 939 F.2d 1106 (CA-5, 1991)

Figlewicz and Sprohge have provided 10 guidelines to help experts avoid legal challenges:[35]

- Know the relevant professional standards.
- Apply the relevant professional standards.
- Know the relevant professional literature.
- Know the relevant professional organizations.
- Use generally accepted analytical methods.
- Use multiple analytical methods.
- Synthesize the conclusions of the multiple analytical methods.
- Disclose all significant analytical assumptions and variables.
- Subject the analysis to peer review.
- Test the analysis – and the conclusions – for reasonableness.
- Obviously, an expert has a great deal of guidelines to follow other than mere technical knowledge.

JUSTIFYING METHODOLOGY

If accountants plan to use a new methodology to analyze a matter at issue, they will have to convince the judge that the new methodology makes sense. Ideally, they will be able to point to other experts who find the new methodology acceptable.

Once accountants have been qualified more than once as an expert witness, *Daubert* challenges are likely to become rarer. More frequently, opposing counsel will be willing to stipulate that they are experts.

Court-Appointed Expert Witnesses

Courts may, on their own motion or on the motion of any party to the litigation appoint an expert witness.[36] Courts may appoint an expert witness agreed upon by the parties or may select their own expert witness.[37]

---

[35] R.E. Figlewicz and Hans-Dieter Sprohge, "The CPA's Expert Witness Role in Litigation Services: A Maze of Legal and Accounting Standards," *The Ohio CPA Journal* (July-September 2002), p. 35.

[36] See, e.g., Rule 706(a) of the Federal Rules of Evidence.

[37] See, e.g., Rule 706(a) of the Federal Rules of Evidence.

That a court appoints an expert witness does not prevent parties from calling expert witnesses of their own selection.[38] An individual may not be appointed as an expert witness unless the individual agrees to act as an expert witness.[39]

An individual appointed by a court as an expert witness will be informed of his or her duties by the court.[40] Court-appointed expert witnesses must advise all parties to the litigation of their findings.[41] They may be deposed by any party and may be called to testify by the court or any party.[42] When testifying, court-appointed experts may be cross-examined by each party, including the party who called the witness.[43]

Court-appointed expert witnesses are entitled to reasonable compensation, whatever sum the court may allow.[44] Their compensation may be paid by the parties in such proportion as the judge directs or from funds provided by law for such purposes.[45]

WEIGHT VERSUS ADMISSIBILITY

There is a difference between using a *Daubert* challenge for admissibility versus weight. *Daubert* analysis should not replace trial on merits, but any defects in an expert's methods should be addressed through cross-examination.[46] The duty of a district court is to ensure that the basis of an expert's opinion is not so fatally flawed as to render his or her opinion inadmissible as matter of law.[47] For example, an appellate court said that the defendant did not argue that the expert fails to comport with *Daubert*

---

[38] See, e.g., Rule 706(d) of the Federal Rules of Evidence.

[39] See, e.g., Rule 706(a) of the Federal Rules of Evidence.

[40] See, e.g., Rule 706(a) of the Federal Rules of Evidence.

[41] See, e.g., Rule 706(a) of the Federal Rules of Evidence.

[42] See, e.g., Rule 706(a) of the Federal Rules of Evidence.

[43] See, e.g., Rule 706(a) of the Federal Rules of Evidence.

[44] See, e.g., Rule 706(b) of the Federal Rules of Evidence.

[45] See, e.g., Rule 706(b) of the Federal Rules of Evidence.

[46] Mathis v. Exxon Corp., 302 F.3d 448 (CA-5, 2002).

[47] Inre Visa Check, 280 F.3d 124 (CA-2, 2001), cert.den. 122 S.Ct. 2382 (2002).

factors, but rather argued that his calculations did not support his conclusion. This attack is not a true *Daubert* challenge, but rather goes to weight.[48]

Creditors argued that a company's quarrels with expert's approach went to weight, not admissibility, but district court identified no fewer than eighteen deficiencies, and testimony was riddled with implausible and unexplained assumptions. The Second Circuit said that there was no abuse of discretion.[49] However, in another situation the Ninth Circuit said that a plaintiff's expert was qualified, and used mathematical extrapolation, straight line linear progression, and averaging to arrive at his figures. Defendants attacked none of these methodologies, and their objections went to weight, not reliability.[50]

Also, the First Circuit said that defendants did not object at the trial court level and so review is for plain error. Defendants said expert is unqualified, but he spent 33 years as an IRS agent, mostly investigating financial fraud. Defendants also fault expert for basing analysis solely on bank records supplied by plaintiffs, rather than broader array of transactions, but this objection goes to weight, not admissibility.[51]

MAINTAINING INDEPENDENCE FROM THE CLIENT

Although accountants serving as a consultant to an attorney may be an advocate for a client, accountants who act as expert witnesses must be concerned about maintaining at least the appearance of independence from their client. Their relationship with a client must not be such that it would lead jurors and judges to question whether they can be impartial and fair in reaching their opinions. For example, accountants should not agree to a fee contingent on the success of their testimony. They should be paid for their time and expenses, not for their opinion.

---

[48] *TFWS v. Schaefer*, 325 F. 3d 234 (CA-4, 2003).

[49] *Lippe v. Bairnco Corp.*, 288 B.R. 678 (S.D. N.Y. 2003), aff.d No. 03-7360 (2nd Cir. Apr. 9, 2004) (unpublished)

[50] *CDM Mfg. v. Complete Sales Representation, Inc.* No. 01-56138 (9th Cir. Oct. 29, 2002) (unpublished).

[51] *Microfinancial, Inc. v. Premier Holidays Int'l, Inc.*, No.04-1493 (1st Cir. Oct 5, 2004).

Lack of independence not only may undermine an expert witness' testimony (and perhaps disqualify the individual from testifying) but also may make an expert witness' working papers with respect to the client and other engagements subject to discovery by the opposing party.

Evidence Upon Which Experts May Rely

Forensic accountants must be familiar with legal concepts and procedures. Nothing spoils a court dispute quicker than lack of evidence, and expert opinions are evidence.[52] Experts may base their opinions on facts or data that they themselves perceived or which were made known to them at or before a judicial hearing.[53] The facts or data need not be admissible in evidence in order for the expert's opinion to be admitted if the facts or data are of a type reasonably relied upon by experts in the same field in forming opinions.[54] Otherwise, inadmissible facts or data may not be disclosed to the jury unless the court determines that their probative value in assisting the jury in evaluating the expert's opinion substantially outweighs their prejudicial effect.[55]

Unless the court requires otherwise, experts need not testify to the facts or data underlying their opinions before giving their opinion and the reasons for their opinion.[56] However, they may be required to disclose underlying facts or data on cross-examination.[57] Although expert witnesses are allowed to present naked opinions, if their testimony has an inadequate foundation, the court can exclude their testimony.

Ghost-Written Reports

An expert report must be prepared by the expert and not by his or her attorney. An expert report prepared mostly from interrogatory answers prepared by the party's lawyers is not sufficient.[58] "Rule 26(a) (2) (B) does

---

[52] D.W. Squires, "Problems Solved With Forensic Accounting: A Legal Perspective," *Journal of Forensic Accounting*, Vol. IV, 2003, p. 132

[53] See, e.g., Rule 703 of the Federal Rules of Evidence

[54] See, e.g., Rule 703 of the Federal Rules of Evidence

[55] See, e.g., Rule 703 of the Federal Rules of Evidence

[56] See, e.g., Rule 705 of the Federal Rules of Evidence

[57] See, e.g., Rule 705 of the Federal Rules of Evidence

[58] FRCP 26(a) (2) (B). *Smith v. State Farm Fire & Cas. Co.*, 164 FRD 49 (SD VA 1995)

not preclude counsel from providing assistance to experts in preparing the reports, and indeed, with experts such as automobile mechanics, this assistance may be needed. Nevertheless, the report, which is intended to set forth the substance of direct examination, should be written in a manner that reflects the testimony to be given by the witness, and it must be signed by the witness."[59]

In one dispute an attorney assisted an expert in preparing a report by providing assistance in retyping and incorporating changes authorized by the expert. A trial attorney "may well have legitimate cause to give assistance to an expert witness in the preparation of the report." But the court also emphasized that in no way does it suggest that the attorneys have license to change the opinions and report of the expert witnesses.[60]

In another dispute an attorney actually wrote the expert report, but the attached opinions and work papers were those of the expert, and the expert testified at deposition that the report reflected his opinions.[61] Still in another case a Virginia court found "significant evidence of teamwork and collaboration between ATE (a government litigation consultant) and the U.S.'s testifying expert." There was "extensive substantive assistance in drafting the expert's report." [62]

In still another dispute an expert report was "substantially derived" from a prior case, which was "substantially similar" to a different expert's report in another dispute. Since there was "substantially similarity among the three expert witness reports derived from the authorship of this common language by plaintiff's counsel, the Michigan court struck an expert's report because it had "not been prepared by the expert" in violation of FRCP 26 (a) (2).[63]

The U.S. Tax Court indicates that certain kinds of help are clearly available to assist an expert. For example, a lawyer's assistance with the preparation of documents required by Rule 26, such as a list of cases in which the

---

[59] Advisory Committee notes to FRCP 26

[60] *Marek v. Moore*, FRD 298 (DKS 1997)

[61] *Indiana Ins. Co. v. Hussey Seating Co.*, 176 FRD 293(D. IN 1997)

[62] *Trigon Insurance Co.*, 88 AFTR 2d 2001-6883 (DC Va.2001)

[63] In re Jackson Natl. Life Ins. Co. Premium Litigation, 1999 WL 33510008 (DC Mich, 1999)

expert has testified, or fine-tuning a disclosure with expert's input to insure that a report compiles with the various rules, is permissible. Preparing an expert's opinion "from whole cloth and then asking the expert to sign it if he or she wishes to adopt it conflicts with Rule 26(a)(2)(B)'s requirement that the expert 'prepare the report.' Preparation implies involvement other than pursuing a report drafted by someone else and placing one's name at the bottom to indicate agreement. In other words, the assistance of counsel contemplated by Rule 26(a)(2)(B) is not synonymous with ghost-writing."[64]

In *Bank One Corporation* the Tax Court rejected a jointly prepared 20-page expert rebuttal report on the behalf of two experts since it was prepared primarily by only one expert and by taxpayer's counsel. The report went through 12 revisions. The Tax Court complained that the expert never explained to their satisfaction that the words, analysis, and opinions in that report were his own work and a reflection of his own expertise. This court was not persuaded that the expert played any meaningful role in preparing the contents of the rebuttal report. "He was vague, uncertain, and unfamiliar with the contents of the report, and he was uncomfortable and evasive, and he was uncomfortable about his role in its preparation."[65]

Hurwitz and Carpenter say that permissible assistance certainly should include familiarizing an expert with the requirements of Tax Court Rule 143(f) (1) and helping the expert understand what information must be included in the expert report. By contrast, an expert's report written entirely by an attorney is automatically suspect. Behavior falling between these two extremes poses more trouble.[66] They assert that it is likely that the U.S. Tax Court will allow an expert to serve as a scribe only when the expert is not capable of articulating his or her thoughts in the form of a written report.[67]

---

[64] *Bank One Corp.* 120 T.C. 174 (2003)

[65] *Bank One Corp.*, 120 TC 174 (2003): Judge Laro's Order dated 1/15/03, page 29.

[66] S.M. Hurwitz and R. Carpenter, "Can An Attorney Participate in the Writing of an 'Expert Witness" Report in the Tax Court?" *Journal of Taxation*, June 2004, pp. 358-362

[67] Ibid.

SIDE-TAKING

Side-taking or result-oriented work may result in a trial judge dismissing an expert. Hints at a lawyer's line of arguments provided before reviewing evidence can influence an accounting expert's decision about an auditor's compliance with GAAS.[68] For example, in a fifty-seven page decision involving the valuation of a company the U.S. Tax Court attacked a valuation expert, Dr. Shannon Pratt.[69] The IRS used as its expert on the valuation questions Dr. Shannon Pratt, managing director of Willamette Management Associates and the acknowledged guru of business appraisers. Tax Court Judge Renato Beghe nevertheless concluded that "Willametie's report was result-oriented and this was reflected in Dr. Pratt's testimony." The Judge noted that appraisers "have third-party responsibilities – just as certified public accountants do – to those who rely on their opinions, and their determinations must be independent and objective..."[70]

The judge said that Dr. Pratt strayed from the standard of objectivity and cast aside his scholar's mantle and became 'a shill' for respondent." Thus, Judge Beghe rejected most of both the Willamette report and Dr. Pratt's testimony, but did take account of Dr. Pratt's criticism of the taxpayer's expert reports and testimony.

CONCLUSION

There are a number of ways for an expert and his or her report to be excluded from the courtroom. *Daubert* and *Frye* challenges are now common hurdles that experts must navigate. Accountants must take the qualification process seriously to avoid adversely affecting their clients and their personal reputation. Lack of independence, conflicts of interest, side-taking, and result-oriented work are situations to avoid. Sarah E. Murray summarizes the expert's paradox as an advocate hired by one party in an

---

[68] D.N. Ricchiute, "Effects of an Attorney's Line of Argument on Accountants' Expert Witness Testimony," *Accounting Review*, January 2004, pp. 221-245.

[69] *Estate of Bessie I. Mueller v. Commissioner*, T.C. Memo. 1992-284, Doc 92-4343

[70] See B.J. Raby and W.L. Raby, "Reasonable Compensation, Expert Witnesses, and the Tax Practitioner," *Tax Notes*, September 15, 2003, p. 1417.

adversarial dispute. However, an expert "will only be persuasive if the jurors or judge believe that you are a neutral and objective expert (like a scientist), with an opinion that has not been influenced by the adversarial nature of the forum."[71]

The AICPA suggests four hold-harmless provisions to be included in engagement letters. Practice Aid 04-1 suggests attaching your curriculum vitae (CV) as an exhibit to the engagement letter, with the following clause:

> As an exhibit to this engagement letter, I have attached my CV. If a court later determines that I am not qualified to offer testimony, such determination will not be deemed a breach of this agreement, and you will still be liable for the payment of fees and expenses as set forth herein.[72]

---

[71] Sarah E. Murray, "Standing At The Crossroads of Truth and Advocacy," NACVA Conference, Miami, June 3, 2004.

[72] C.L. Wilkins and J.H. Kinrich, Business Valuation/Forensic and Litigation Services Practice Aid 04-1, "Engagement Letters in Litigation Services," a practice aid issued by the AICPA Forensic and Litigation Service Committee.

CHAPTER 6

Advocacy and the Expert Witness

William M. Michaelson

One of the most critical issues in a litigation engagement is advocacy on the part of an expert witness. As part of the pre-engagement process the role of the expert in relation to advocacy must be clearly understood. This understanding will allow an expert to determine in advance those situations which allow advocacy so as to maximize service to the client.

Objectivity is a critical element when appearing before a trier of fact whether it be a judge or a jury. Cases are lost when a judge or jury believes that an expert appears to be an advocate whereby the opinions are prejudiced in favor of the client. The expert's credibility is rendered moot and the client's case is compromised. The appearance of advocacy can take many forms whether it be financial, personal or other.

Advocacy on the part of an expert does not always carry a negative aura. This article explores not only the negative – it also discusses situations where advocacy is positive and can benefit a case. The expert must understand his or her role in the case and determine how the appearance of advocacy will affect the case and is appropriate.

CPA, experts can be categorized into three groups:

- Testifying Experts
- Consulting Experts
- Fact Witnesses

William M. Michaelson CPA, CFE, MAE, DABFA is president of Michaelson & Co., P.A. in West Palm Beach, Florida. Mr. Michaelson practices nationally, extensively in the areas of litigation support and forensic accounting in criminal, commercial and marital matters. He is on the editorial review committee of the *Journal of Forensic Accounting* and authors numerous articles and speaks nationally on such matters.

As previously discussed, at the onset of an expert's involvement in a case it is essential that the attorney, client and the CPA decide which category the CPA falls into. Typically, an expert will not fall within more than one of these categories. In rare instances, an expert may be a fact witness as well as one of the other categories. This must be extensively explained prior to the engagement. Being a fact witness and a consulting witness is more common. In extremely rare instances there are situations where a fact witness appears as an expert, however, this is not recommended, and if employed prior stipulation of counsel must be obtained.

TESTIFYING EXPERT

The role of the testifying expert is to appear before a trier of fact and render an opinion either by deposition or courtroom testimony. This is the typical role required of most CPA experts. The goal of this testimony is to assist the trier of fact in understanding the matters relating to the matter before the court. As part of the discovery process, prior to an appearance in court, a testifying expert's opinions and work product in support of his or her opinion is discoverable through the deposition process. This process assists both sides to flush out strengths and weaknesses in their respective cases and can expedite a settlement or allow the respective testifying experts to modify their positions accordingly utilizing the facts and circumstances discovered.

Whether an expert is a testifying, consulting or a fact witness, as a CPA they must conform to the Rules of Professional Conduct of the American Institute of Certified Public Accountants (AICPA). Other non-CPA organizations have similar standards for their members to adhere to. For instance, Rule 102 of the AICPA Code of Professional Conduct states, "In the performance of any professional services, a member shall maintain objectivity and integrity, shall be free of conflicts of interest, and shall not knowingly misrepresent facts or subordinate his or her judgment to others." This rule goes to the heart of the advocacy issue that a testifying expert must address in the performance of their duties.

There exists exceptions to the rule involving conflicts of interest. Applying the exceptions, one could conclude that a testifying expert could perform services for a client even though a conflict of interest exists as long as 1) the practitioner believes the service can be performed with objectivity, 2) the party entitled to the confidential treatment, or potentially disadvantaged by the conflict of interest, the opposition, is made aware of the conflict, and 3) that party waives the conflict. Having said that, a testifying expert must tread very carefully when applying these exceptions.

Other rules contained in the Code of Professional Conduct should also be considered by any CPA or non-CPA expert as they address other issues that go to the very core of the advocacy issue. Besides integrity and objectivity addressed in Rule 102, Rule 101 and 302 play an important role in the question of advocacy by a testifying expert. Rule 101 requires the expert to be independent. This matter goes back to the heart of Rule 102 incorporating the issues of conflicts of interest discussed above. The issue at hand is that each organization an expert belongs to may have a different, more stringent, interpretation of the same issue resulting in a completely different behavior on the part of the expert.

Rule 302, contingent fees provides that, "in most cases, professional services should not be rendered under an agreement whereby the fee is contingent on the findings or results of services." The rule is administered differently in various states. The safest fee arrangement where advocacy is at question is an hourly fee for services rendered.

During the deposition process a testifying expert must be prepared to answer questions relating to the above standards when the opposition is ferreting out any issues that are discussed above involving advocacy in relation to a testifying expert. The structure of a retainer letter, which most surely will be required to be produced, will address many of the above issues. *It is, therefore, advisable to take great care in the preparation of the written understanding between the testifying expert and the client to avoid the advocacy issues.*

It is also important to remember advocacy is not just how an expert comes across on the stand but how he or she conducts themselves prior to testimony.

Now having addressed some of the administrative issues concerning advocacy and the testifying expert, let us turn our attention to the technical issues and how they are presented.

A testifying expert will most certainly lose credibility when attempting to advocate an issue by defending an opinion that has been successfully challenged during the cross examination process. Keeping in mind that in a deposition conducted by opposing counsel, the information sought is not only the expert opinions and how they were derived, but also whether there are opinions contrary to those of an opposing expert. During the deposition process the expert may be asked a series of hypothetical questions that are intended to cast doubt with a trier of fact as to whether the expert has become an advocate and thereby lost his or her objectivity.

When giving testimony at trial, any errors in math or interpretation of facts that have been discovered during the deposition process or while on the stand should be admitted to in an effort to repair the testimony and provide a suitable explanation. It is acceptable and even encouraged to admit any mistakes and repair previously given testimony instead of becoming defensive and attempting to support a position that is indefensible. Such behavior can discredit the entire testimony, even issues that may be correct. Often a trier of fact is dispelled from believing an expert has become an advocate when an admission of error or a reasonable explanation is provided.

Other examples of how an expert may demonstrate their independence and objectivity are:

1. Using information that is not at the extreme end of a range (i.e. only when it benefits their client's position) when the facts of the case and the resultant opinions require the utilization of ranges or other variables. If a range is necessary to utilize, be fair and utilize conservatism in your judgment.

2. Include all of the data available even if it is provided by the opposing expert or litigant. Do not "cherry pick" information that only benefits your client's position. Too often an expert's opinion and presentation is discredited when opposing counsel can show that if an expert utilized known facts an extremely different conclusion would be warranted.

The expert's evidence should be, and should be seen to be, the independent product of the expert, uninfluenced as to form or content of the litigation. After evaluating the facts, a testifying expert may come to the realization that a position a lawyer wants him or her to support is entirely impossible to defend. It must be kept in mind that an attorney is supposed to take the position of an advocate on behalf of his client. Once it is determined that a position proposed is indefensible the testifying expert should immediately inform counsel. This is not to say that there are not alternative positions that may have merit that are supported by the facts and that the expert and attorney need to explore these alternatives.

When providing expert testimony an expert must keep in mind that the theories and practices he or she bases their conclusion and opinions on must successfully withstand a challenge under the *Daubert* Rule. Although this rule applies to federal cases many states have adopted this or a similar approach when dealing with scientific or technical data and the application of such to the formulation of an expert opinion. Simply stated the utilization of theories, methods, positions and the like that are not supported by the standard utilized by those in the industry could end up being inadmissible in court. A testifying expert that ignores the *Daubert* Rule and similar case ideals may appear to be an advocate and endanger his client's case.

CONSULTING EXPERT

As stated previously, the Code of Professional Conduct of whatever organization that an expert holds a credential under apply to consulting experts as well.

There is a great distinction between a testifying expert and a consulting expert. Consulting experts may consult on the attorney's work product, i.e. materials the attorney prepares as background for a case. In this capacity, the consulting expert is in a position similar to that of an associate of the attorney and thereby coming under the privilege rules protecting the consulting expert's work product.

Once an expert is engaged as a witness and begins formulating opinions as part of the case before the court the privilege is waived and the information to be provided by that expert is discoverable, thus becoming a testifying expert. Simply stated, when acting as an expert witness, he or she is bringing official information to the court and so must disclose any contact with the case. When experts act as consultants for attorney's, they are only assisting the attorney and do not have to disclose their involvement in the case. A consulting expert can act as an advocate.

The typical role of a consulting advocate is to provide recommendations for calculations, insight in to a particular industry and standards utilized within that industry, performance of analytical procedures related to the case and any other assistance determined by the attorney and the testifying expert to be necessary. The work of the consulting expert can be incorporated into the opinions of the testifying expert provided the testifying expert is comfortable opining on the information provided. The testifying expert merely educates the court utilizing the facts accumulated and renders his opinions from those facts.

In many instances there can be several testifying experts and consultants used in various combinations depending on the complexity of the matters before the court. As an example, an economic consulting expert may be utilized to accumulate relevant statistical information about a particular industry and feed that information to a testifying expert for utilization in various calculations incorporating the statistical information with raw data specifically derived from the facts at hand.

A consulting expert may also be utilized to test the calculations, methods and opinions to be put forth by the testifying expert. As a consulting expert he or she owes objectivity to the client and not the court and can advocate his or her position on their client's behalf. This becomes a useful tool by the testifying expert in preparing for all contingencies related to the case. The consulting expert plays the role of devil's advocate ferreting out any inconsistencies that may exist is his client's case as well as the opposition's case.

FACT WITNESSES

Accountants may be called to testify as a fact witness in a matter before the court. They are called upon to testify solely regarding factual information relating to a case and are not expected to render any expert opinions. Just as testifying and consulting experts must adhere to the Code of Conduct as discussed previously, so must a fact witness/CPA or other professional.

An example of a fact witness in a financial case, the client's bookkeeper whether internal or external may be called upon to testify as to the content of the books and records utilized by a testifying expert in the formulation of his or her opinions. In light of the specific nature of their testimony as it relates to specific facts, advocacy is usually not a problem since no opinions are to be rendered.

As discussed previously, a fact witness may be called upon to serve as a consulting expert or even a testifying expert. The objectivity and integrity of the fact witness still comes in to question as they most certainly will be characterized by the opposition as being biased in the utilization of the data that they alone were responsible for.

GUIDANCE

The role of each expert on the team should be determined by the attorney from the onset of the case. To assist the expert there are many publications provided by various professional industry groups that assist in explaining an expert's role in a case and the rules to follow to assure that no damage is created by his or her representation.

This is very true in light of those rare situations where even a consulting expert may be called to testify, therefore waiving the privacy rules and thereby causing his or her role and information to become discoverable. Since such a situation could cause a significant problem in the case. Every effort to avoid this should be made by discussing this with the attorney and developing a strategy to effectively handle the situation.

As one can see, advocacy can crop up in various forms, therefore preplanning and understanding an expert's role as it relates to the matter at hand must be addressed early on in the case with the litigation team led by the attorney.

CHAPTER 7

A Case Study of the Role of the Forensic Accountant in a Legal Dispute

Thomas A. Buckhoff and **Mark H. Taylor**

With increasing frequency, forensic accountants are called upon to play important roles in resolving legal disputes ranging from civil actions such as breaches of fiduciary duty to Racketeer Influenced Corrupt Organizations (RICO) Act criminal violations involving gambling, arson for profit, extortion, securities fraud, and mail fraud. In any litigation, the forensic accountant's role is to examine the financial issues relevant to the case, summarize and explain those issues to interested parties (e.g. the judge, attorneys and plaintiffs/defendants), and offer expert testimony in court, if necessary. Ultimately, the opinions of the forensic accountant must be presented in a written report that will be reviewed by the opposing parties in the dispute as well as by the judge likely to hear the case. Thus, the report supplies the basis for pre-trial settlement negotiations and in-court testimony if the case does not settle. The report's strength (or lack thereof) also influences the opposition in deciding whether to settle out of court or to 'fight' the matter in court. Consequently, the forensic accountant's report is vital to the successful resolution of a legal dispute. The purpose of this paper is to illustrate the importance and significance of the forensic accountant's report using an actual report that prompted the successful settlement of a $1.7 million lawsuit. The paper also suggests an overall organization to such a report. Together, these illustrations will provide academics with access to an actual forensic accountant's report for purposes of instructing students in the development and use of such reports, as well as a basis for preparing such reports as opportunities to participate in similar cases arise. Suggestions for using the case as an instructional tool are provided in an appendix.

Thomas A. Buckhoff, Ph.D., CPA, CFE is Associate Professor of Forensic Accounting at Georgia Southern University, Statesboro, GA. Mark H. Taylor, Ph.D., CPA is John P. Begley Endowed Chair in Accounting at Creighton University, Omaha, NE.

INTRODUCTION

Recent accounting frauds such as those involving Arthur Andersen, Dynegy, Enron, Global Crossing, K-Mart, Merck, Qwest, Tyco, WorldCom, and Xerox and numerous others have wiped out tens of billions of dollars in shareholder value and has placed forensic accounting and forensic accountants in the spotlight more than ever before. A feature story from U.S. News & World Report described forensic accountants as "the bloodhounds of bookkeeping [who] sniff out fraud and criminal transactions in corporate financial records." The story listed the "forensic accountant" as the first of "eight of the nation's most secure career tracks" (Levine, 2002). Statement on Auditing Standard (SAS) Number 99—Consideration of Fraud in a Financial Statement Audit and the Sarbanes-Oxley Act of 2002 are forcing companies to more aggressively seek out fraud. Boards of directors are demanding that forensic accounting become part of corporate governance and of financial reporting. Consequently, top accounting firms predict forensic accounting services to increase by as much as 50% (Iwata, 2003).

An increasingly common service provided by forensic accountants is the preparation of reports that summarize and defend the findings of a forensic engagement in which they have been involved. Such reports play an important role, not only in the completion of forensic engagements, but also in subsequent litigation. Few, if any, examples of such reports based on real-world fraud examinations are available. The purpose of this paper is to help fill that void by explaining both the importance and significance of the report itself, and to present an example of such a report derived from actual litigation involving a RICO[1] violation. The expert report was used to successfully resolve a $1.7 million lawsuit. The next section provides necessary background by examining the role of the forensic accountant in a legal dispute.

---

[1] The RICO statute was originally enacted in 1970 to fight organized crime's infiltration of legitimate business; however, its powerful criminal and civil provisions have come to be used in a wide range of fraud cases. The statute outlaws the investment of ill-gotten gains in another business enterprise, the acquisition of an interest in an enterprise through certain illegal acts, and/or the conduct of the affairs of an enterprise through such acts. Under RICO, private individuals may recover three times their actual loss, plus attorneys' fees, for economic damages caused by a violation of the statute.

Role of the Forensic Accountant in a Legal Dispute

With increasing frequency, forensic accountants assist attorneys in litigation involving matters such as financial frauds, embezzlements, misappropriation of funds, arson for profit, bankruptcy fraud, deceptive accounting practices, professional negligence, and tax evasion. Such assistance typically takes one of two forms: consulting expert or testifying expert. Both types of experts provide background information for developing litigation strategy, prepare written opinions, advise on depositions, and respond to discovery requests. Accordingly, they review documents, transactions, and other financial records to: (1) uncover the details of any defalcation, (2) establish responsibility for it, and (3) estimate losses incurred as a result of the defalcation. However, the consulting expert typically is much closer to the matter under dispute and has a much deeper understanding of it than does the testifying expert. For example, the consulting expert may know of fraud theories for which no corroborating evidence could be found whereas the testifying expert will only learn of the successful fraud theories. As long as consulting experts do not testify in court and are engaged directly by the attorney, their work product is protected by attorney-client privilege and is not subject to discovery by the opposition (Babitsky et. al., 2000).

The testifying expert performs many of the same functions as the consulting expert but also provides expert testimony in court. Before testifying in court the testifying expert must first be 'qualified' or accepted by the court as an expert witness. To establish their expertise to the judge and jury, testifying experts respond to questions concerning their professional credentials, which typically encompass education, work experience, licensing or certification, technical training, books and journal articles written, offices held in professional associations, awards and commendations received. Since many legal disputes become a battle of expert witnesses, it is advantageous to engage an experienced testifying expert with strong professional credentials. After being qualified, the testifying expert must educate the jury by: (1) establishing the facts, (2) interpreting the facts, and (3) commenting on the opposing expert's facts and opinions (ACFE, 2003). Since the work product of testifying experts is subject to discovery by the opposition, attorneys will not provide them with information they do not want discovered by the opposition.

Forensic accountants may be engaged by the plaintiff/prosecution, defense, or by the court to educate the judge about fraud-related matters relevant to the matter under dispute. Each of these roles demands certain prerequisites and logistics in terms of the forensic accountant's skill set but also in terms of the relevant tasks that they must accomplish. For example, forensic accountants must understand and have the ability to properly document and report the findings resulting from their investigative efforts. When serving as a testifying expert, such documentation becomes even more important as the opposing parties will scrutinize, in minute detail, the content of such a report seeking material for rebuttal, contradiction, and embarrassment. Hence, the expert report is an extremely important document that merits attention in the literature.

THE EXPERT REPORT

In most cases, experts must document their opinions and the evidence underlying them in a written report. Such expert reports may be required for a variety of reasons. First, a written report may be required by the court pursuant to Federal Rule of Civil Procedure 26(2)(B). Second, the expert report may provide the script for the expert's testimony in court. Third, the expert report may be used to counter a *Motion for Summary Judgment*[2] or to discourage the opposition from demanding a costly deposition of the expert. Finally, a well-written and soundly reasoned report may prompt the opposition to concede during out-of-court settlement negotiations. Whatever the reason, the expert's report plays a crucial role in resolving legal disputes and should be carefully drafted (Babitsky, 2000).

The Association of Certified Fraud Examiners offers the following suggestions for preparing an effective expert report (ACFE, 2003):

- Be brief.
- Avoid ambiguity, inexact language, or technical language.
- Avoid generalizations; be specific.

---

[2] A pre-trial Motion for Summary Judgment can be made by either side in a civil dispute. Such a motion petitions the judge to decide the case, without a trial, based on the evidence in the plaintiff's complaint and the defendant's answer. The motion is granted unless either side disputes the facts as presented by the other side.

- Add charts or graphs where appropriate.
- Reference your work.
- Meticulously check the report for accuracy and neatness.

When preparing the expert report, keep in mind that the opposing counsel will carefully scrutinize the report looking for anything that might diminish the expert's credibility in the eyes of the court. The following case study illustrates the role of the forensic accountant in a legal dispute as both a consulting expert and a testifying expert. In addition, the related expert report (see Exhibit 2) exemplifies many of the characteristics of effective expert reports.

A CASE STUDY OF A LEGAL DISPUTE[3]

Background

For over 25 years Thomas Burns had owned and managed a number of successful restaurant franchises located in the Upper-Midwest and Canada. He had a reputation as an aggressive businessman who delegated to others the day-to-day operations of his various business ventures. Thomas had been especially successful at selecting and purchasing ideal restaurant locations before the local real estate market recognized and charged a premium for those locations. However, he rarely put much of his own money at risk in these business ventures, but preferred to finance these ventures with other people's money. In his spare time Thomas had obtained a private pilot's license and purchased a 1992 Piper Seneca III that he used for both business and leisure purposes. With the consent of his tax accountant, he wrote off the entire $358,000 cost of the aircraft as a business expense.

Regarding his personal life, Thomas was married with two children who, after graduating from Ivy-league universities, had moved to Southern California to establish professional careers. Thomas and his wife enjoyed living a comfortable, even extravagant, lifestyle. They lived in a beautiful

---

[3] The names of investigators, forensic accountants, plaintiffs, defendants, and related entities have all been changed to preserve confidentiality. For additional background details, see the Appendix for a factual summary of the case as prepared by plaintiff's attorneys.

home, drove expensive cars, dined at the finest restaurants, and frequently took vacations to exotic places. In addition, they generously shared their wealth with their children and friends. Rumor had it that Thomas kept exactly $100,000 cash stashed in a safe in his home "for a rainy day" and enjoyed showing it to visitors.

Lou Erickson was a retired businessman who had spent 30+ years of his career in upper-management positions at *Fortune* 500 corporations. He knew most, if not all, of the accounting tricks that were used to put a 'positive spin' on financial statements. Consequently, he did not trust the stock market and chose not to invest there. Instead, Lou preferred to create and invest in business ventures that he had carefully selected and researched and then let others run the business. In early 1995 Lou invited several friends and former business associates to a social at his home. After some mingling and socializing, Lou presented a business proposition to them: Open two new locations of the popular "Franchise Restaurant" chain that was distinguished not by its food but instead by the attractive, scantily-clad young women it hired to serve the predominantly male clientele. The start-up costs for the two ventures would be about $1.75 million. Lou proposed setting up two limited partnerships to finance the start up costs of the restaurants, one of which would be located in Minnesota and the other in Canada. Based on financial information provided by the franchisor, Lou estimated that the limited partners should recover their investments in less than five years. A general partner would need to be selected to manage the day-to-day operations of the two restaurants. The proposition was favorably received and two people suggested Thomas Burns as a potential general manager. Lou offered to approach Thomas about the proposition.

Lou scheduled a business lunch with Thomas for the following week. During the lunch, Lou presented his business proposition and invited Thomas to be the general partner. Unbeknownst to Lou or any of the prospective limited partners, Thomas was having serious cash flow problems caused by a combination of his extravagant lifestyle and some ill-chosen restaurant ventures that were consuming large amounts of his cash. Lou's business proposition came just in time to rescue Thomas from his deteriorating financial situation. Consequently, Thomas readily accepted the proposition and agreed to make the minimum 1% investment (i.e.

$17,500) legally required of general partners in limited partnerships. Eight limited partners, including Lou, agreed to invest $216,562 each to complete the financing to start up the two restaurants.

In March of 1996 Thomas Burns created a corporation that he named Flying High, Inc. to act as the General Partner in the Limited Partnerships that would own the two Franchise Restaurants. He also selected MTC, Inc., a restaurant management company owned and managed by him, to manage the finances of the two restaurants and appointed Alan Kirk to be the general manager of both. After much pre-opening publicity and fanfare, the two restaurants opened and for the first two years attracted better-than-expected numbers of customers. However, despite strong restaurant traffic, the restaurants failed to generate positive cash flow available for distribution to the limited partners. Instead, to cover the restaurants' losses, the limited partners were periodically issued "cash calls" that required them to invest more money into the restaurants with the promise that things would improve shortly. Contrary to the provisions of the partnership agreement, the limited partners were not provided financial statements or any financial information to justify the need for the cash calls. Understandably dismayed, the limited partners demanded financial statements so they could evaluate how their substantial cash investments were being managed. MTC, Inc. was contractually responsible for producing the financial statements but consistently stonewalled numerous requests by the limited partners for financial statements. Consequently, the dissident limited partners, led by Lou Erickson, filed a civil lawsuit against Thomas Burns and related parties claiming mail and wire fraud and violations of the Racketeer Influenced Corrupt Organizations (RICO) statute. Exhibit 1 presents a visual diagram of the various parties involved in the legal dispute.

Resolving the Legal Dispute

To assist in resolving the dispute between the dissident limited partners and Thomas Burns, the plaintiffs' attorneys engaged the professional firm Woodruff & Associates, LLP, a firm that specialized in fraud detection, investigation, and prevention consulting services. The firm then assigned Bill Benson, a certified fraud examiner and retired federal agent, to work as a consulting expert on the case. Mr. Benson first met with the attorneys and the limited partners to develop a strategy for collecting and examining the documents and financial records needed to resolve the allegations under dispute. Subsequently, Mr. Benson organized and examined over 28,000 documents and identified 20 incidents of fraud in a written report to plaintiff's attorneys. The consulting firm then assigned Winston Woodruff – a partner in the firm who possessed a Ph.D. and was a certified public accountant (CPA) and a certified fraud examiner (CFE) – to serve as the testifying expert for the case. Dr. Woodruff met with the attorneys and Mr. Benson, and carefully reviewed Mr. Benson's report along with relevant supporting documentation. Dr. Woodruff then prepared an expert report summarizing and defending his opinion concerning the financial issues under dispute (see Exhibit 2). The rationale for using two different experts in this case is twofold. First, as a consulting expert engaged directly by the attorneys, Mr. Benson's work product and extensive involvement in the case was protected by the attorney-client privilege and was not discoverable by the defendant's attorneys. Second, Dr. Woodruff's extensive academic and professional credentials greatly enhanced his credibility as a testifying expert. Moreover, since Dr. Woodruff was expected to testify in court, his work product and involvement in the case were discoverable by the opposition. However, Dr. Woodruff's limited involvement in the case effectively shielded much information from being discovered by the other side.

Trials substantially increase the litigation costs of the parties caught up in a legal dispute. Consequently, few civil lawsuits ever go to trial. Most cases either settle prior to trial or are otherwise disposed of through pretrial motions (Kramer & Connolly, 2005). Thus, the expert report will most likely be used to motivate the other side to reach a favorable out-of-court settlement. Perceived weaknesses in the expert report can have at least two outcomes detrimental to the client: (1) the other side might decide to go to trial expecting that they can win by exploiting the weaknesses, or (2) the other side might exploit the weaknesses to settle for a lesser amount. In the lawsuit against Thomas E. Burns, the expert report was a major factor in negotiating a favorable out-of-court settlement. After reviewing the expert report in preparation for pre-trial settlement negotiations the judge declared to the plaintiffs, "You have valid fraud claims, and if this goes to trial, you will win." The financial details of the subsequent settlement were kept confidential, even from the forensic accountants who worked as expert witnesses on the case.

CONCLUSION

Forensic accountants are increasingly being called upon to provide litigation support services. In a legal dispute, the forensic accountant's role is to examine the financial issues relevant to the case, summarize and explain those issues to interested parties (e.g. the judge, attorneys and plaintiffs/defendants), and offer expert testimony in court, if necessary. Ultimately, the findings and opinions of the forensic accountant must be presented in a written report that will be reviewed by the opposing parties in the dispute as well as by the judge likely to hear the case. Thus, the expert report provides the basis for pre-trial settlement negotiations and in-court testimony if the case does not settle. The strength of the expert report (or lack thereof) directly influences the opposition in deciding whether to settle out of court or to 'fight' the matter in a trial. Consequently, the forensic accountant's expert report is vital to the successful resolution of a legal dispute.

REFERENCES

Association of Certified Fraud Examiners (ACFE). 2003. *Fraud Examiners Manual*: 2.701, 2.704.

Babitsky, S, J. Mangraviti, and C. Todd. 2000. *The Comprehensive Forensic Services Manual: The Essential Resources for all Experts*. Seak, Inc.: 260, 127-129.

Iwata, E. (2003). Accounting Detectives in Demand. *USA Today*, (February 28): B03.

Kramer & Connolly. 2005. http://www.kramerslaw.com/step7.htm

Levine, S. (2002). Careers to Count On. *U.S. News & World Report*, (February 18): 46.

Exhibit 1

Woodruff & Associates, LLP
Specializing in Fraud Detection, Investigation, and Prevention Consulting Services

Eagle Gate Towers, Suite 1200
7874 East Superior Road
Richland, IN 48267-2934

Memo

To: Richard Robertson, Lead Prosecutor
From: Winston A. Woodruff, Ph.D., CPA, CFE
Date: January 22, 2002
Subject: Expert report regarding litigation against Thomas E. Burns

Background

Accounting is an information system that identifies, records, and communicates the financial events of an enterprise to interested users. The objectives of financial reporting[4] are to provide:

- information that is useful in investment and credit decisions,
- information that is useful in assessing cash flow prospects, and
- information about enterprise resources, claims to those resources, and changes in them.

To satisfy the above three objectives, a single set of general-purpose financial statements is prepared. These statements are expected to present fairly, clearly, and completely the financial operations of the enterprise. To ensure that financial

---

[4] "Objectives of Financial Reporting by Business Enterprises," *Statement of Financial Accounting Concepts No. 1* (Stamford, Conn.: FASB, November 1978), pars. 5-8.

statements are fairly and accurately presented, the accounting profession has developed standards or rules that should be universally applied. These standards and procedures are called generally accepted accounting principles (GAAP). The term "generally accepted" means either that an authoritative accounting rule-making body has established a principle of reporting in a given area or that over time a given practice has been generally accepted because of its universal application. To understand the importance of having generally accepted "rules" for financial reporting, consider the importance of generally accepted rules in a sport such as football. Without rules, football would be a chaotic mass of confusion. One team might field twenty players while the other only fields ten. One team might award themselves ten points for scoring a touchdown while the other might only award six. One team might condone "facemasking" while the other does not. Without rules, there would be no way to determine whether a team is cheating or which team won the game. Clearly, generally accepted rules are necessary to ensure "fair play" and to be able to determine who won or lost the game.

Without accounting rules, financial reporting would be a chaotic mass of confusion. One business might decide to record sales when the customer agrees to buy and another might decide to record sales when cash is collected. One business might value its property, plant, and equipment at historical cost while another does it at fair market value. One business might reduce the value of its investments to market value while others do not. Without accounting standards, investors, creditors, or other users of accounting information would have an extremely difficult time understanding the substance of a given set of financial statements. Without accounting rules, it would be difficult to determine whether management and employees of a business have "cheated" by diverting some profits to their own pockets and the cost of capital would skyrocket. Clearly, accounting rules are necessary to ensure "fair play" and to provide investors and creditors with fair and accurate information for making investing and lending decisions.

Those charged with managing the day-to-day operating activities of a business have a fiduciary duty[5] to know, and to play by, the "rules" for identifying, recording, summarizing, and communicating financial information. Further, management has a fiduciary duty to establish an accounting system that safeguards business assets from employee theft, robbery, and unauthorized use.

---

[5] Management owes certain duties imposed by law to the owners of the business. The principal fiduciary duties are loyalty and care.

Expert Witness Conclusions

Bill Benson – a senior investigator of Woodruff & Associates, LLP – prepared an investigative report dated November 30, 2001 that presents evidence regarding the formation, operation, and management of Northern Lights Investment Limited Partnership (Northern Lights) and Midwestern Lights Investment Limited Partnership (Midwestern Lights) by Flying Sly, Inc. (Flying Sly) through Thomas Burns; Rochelle Bowman; Vivian Bowman; William Richardson; and Vernon Frankl; MTC, Ltd.; Eastern Lights Ltd.; and Western Wings Investment Limited Partnership during the period November 1995 to January 1999. After reviewing Mr. Benson's investigative report that is based on the information available to date, I have formulated opinions that are based on a reasonable degree of academic and professional certainty. Accordingly, it is my opinion that the following investigative findings constitute either violations of generally accepted accounting principles or breaches of fiduciary duty:

Economic Entity Assumption Violations

The economic entity assumption presumes that the boundaries among economic entities be clearly drawn and maintained such that the activities of a given entity be accounted for separately and distinctly from the activities of all other economic entities. Limited Partnership shares are registered securities, governed by the terms of the Partnership Agreement. The economic entities relevant to this dispute are as follows:

- Northern Lights Investment Limited Partnership (Northern Lights)
- Midwestern Lights Investment Limited Partnership (Midwestern Lights)
- Flying Sly, Inc. (Flying Sly)
- MTC, Ltd.
- Eastern Lights Ltd.
- Western Wings Investment Limited Partnership
- Domestic Beef Company
- Everett Crawford

Regarding the above entities, note that Northern Lights and Midwestern Lights are separate and distinct limited partnerships. Several limited partner investors are common to both partnerships, but not all. The remaining entities are all owned and/or controlled by Thomas Burns. Regardless, the boundaries among the entities must be drawn and maintained such that a proper accounting between each entity and its environment can be effected.

In my opinion, which is based on a reasonable degree of academic and professional certainty, the following investigative findings constitute a blurring of the boundaries among what are supposed to be separate and distinct entities. In essence, violations of this generally accepted accounting principle known as the economic entity assumption:

a. *Timothy Benning, P.C. Invoices*
Northern Lights paid the legal fees and costs necessary to incorporate Flying Sly, Inc. Since Flying Sly – which is wholly owned by Thomas Burns– is a separate economic entity from Northern Lights, this violates the economic entity assumption. Accordingly, any monetary transfers from Northern Lights to Flying Sly that are not authorized by Northern Lights limited partners constitute misappropriations of partnership assets.

These payments also violate Section 4.3, Part (iii) of the Partnership Agreement, which specifically prohibits "any assets of the Partnership to become commingled with the assets of the General Partner as Manager."

b. *Impoundment Agreements*
Funds collected from the limited partners to finance the start up costs of the two restaurants were subject to the provisions of an Impoundment Agreement as required by the State Securities Commission. Such an agreement requires that the invested funds be first deposited into an escrow account until all of the funds needed have been collected, after which the funds are released. Since the impoundment agreements were between Northern Lights and State Bank and Midwestern Lights and State Bank, upon termination of the impoundment agreements the funds should have been deposited into separate Northern Lights and Midwestern Lights bank accounts pursuant to the specific written instructions of the State Securities Commission. Instead, Thomas Burns deposited the funds into a Flying Fly checking account at State Bank. Since Flying Sly – wholly owned by Thomas Burns – is a separate economic entity from Northern Lights and Midwestern Lights, this violates the impoundment agreement, state securities laws, and the economic entity assumption. Accordingly, any funds deposited into a Flying Sly checking account constitute a misappropriation of partnership assets.

These deposits violate Section 4.3, Part (iii) of the Partnership Agreement, which specifically prohibits "any assets of the Partnership to become commingled with the assets of the General Partner as Manager."

c.   *$109,000 Wire Transfer to Trenton, Indiana*

In April 1997, Rochelle Bowman wire transferred $109,000 from the Flying Sly, Inc. checking account at State Bank to Trenton, Indiana to finance the construction of a restaurant (i.e. Domestic Beef) being built by Thomas Burns. No receivable was ever established on the books of Midwestern Lights. Since the only funds in the Flying Sly checking account at the time were Midwestern Lights investor funds and the restaurant was a separate economic entity owned by Thomas Burns and others not partners in Midwestern Lights or Northern Lights, this violates the economic entity assumption. Since Flying Sly – wholly owned by Thomas Burns – is a separate economic entity from Midwestern Lights, this violates the economic entity assumption. Accordingly, the $109,000 wire transfer constitutes a misappropriation of partnership assets.

This transaction violates Section 4.3, Part (iii) of the Partnership Agreement, which specifically prohibits "any assets of the Partnership to become commingled with the assets of the General Partner as Manager." In addition, it violates Section 4.3, Part (ii) of the Partnership Agreement, which specifically prohibits the lending of "any assets of the Partnership to or guarantee any obligations of the General Partner, as Manager."

d.   *Commingling-Flying Sly and Northern Lights/Midwestern Lights*

Funds received by both Northern Lights and Midwestern Lights from the sale of the unauthorized Canadian calendars, nylons, uniforms, and gift certificates were deposited into Flying Sly checking accounts. Since Flying Sly – wholly owned by Thomas Burns – is a separate economic entity from Northern Lights and Midwestern Lights, this violates the economic entity assumption. Accordingly, any such funds deposited into Flying Sly checking accounts should be considered a misappropriation of partnership assets.

These deposits violate Section 4.3, Part (iii) of the Partnership Agreement, which specifically prohibits "any assets of the Partnership to become commingled with the assets of the General Partner as Manager."

e.   *Payments to Bernard Macintosh*

Legal costs incurred in 1997 by defendants for the establishment of a Crimson Rose Restaurant were paid for with Northern Lights funds and never repaid by Calgary. Since the Crimson Rose Restaurant is a separate economic entity from Northern

Lights and Midwestern Lights, this violates the economic entity assumption. Accordingly, any legal costs related to the Crimson Rose paid for with Northern Lights funds should be considered a misappropriation of partnership assets.

These payments violate Section 4.3, Part (iii) of the Partnership Agreement, which specifically prohibits "any assets of the Partnership to become commingled with the assets of the General Partner as Manager."

f.   Crimson Rose Restaurant

During 1998, Midwestern Lights and Northern Lights assets including things such as gift certificates, dolphin shorts, golf shirts, tee shirts, booster seats, tracksuits, employee lockers, and calendars were transferred to the Crimson Rose Restaurant. Since these asset transfers were not approved by the Midwestern Lights and Northern Lights investors and the Crimson Rose Restaurant is a separate economic entity from Midwestern Lights and Northern Lights, this violates the economic entity assumption. Accordingly, any such unauthorized transfers of assets constitute misappropriations of partnership assets.

Vernon Frankl and William Richardson were both paid full-time salaries as employees of Northern Lights yet "spent a lot of time working on the Crimson Rose." Justine Wilson stated that "Crimson Rose Restaurant and the calendar occupied about 60 percent of Richardson's time." Such activities were not approved by, nor did they benefit, Northern Lights investors. Since the Crimson Rose is a separate economic entity from Northern Lights, this violates the economic entity assumption. Accordingly, a misappropriation of partnership assets has occurred when Vernon Frankl and/or William Richardson were working at the Crimson Rose while they were full-time employees of Northern Lights and Midwestern Lights.

These transactions and activities violate Section 4.3, Part (iii) of the Partnership Agreement, which specifically prohibits "any assets of the Partnership to become commingled with the assets of the General Partner as Manager." In addition, such activity violates Section 4.3, Part (ii) of the Partnership Agreement, which specifically prohibits the lending of "any assets of the Partnership to or guarantee any obligations of the General Partner, as Manager."

1.   Related Party Disclosure Violations

Statement of Financial Accounting Standards (SFAS) No. 57 entitled "Related Party Disclosures" [6] defines related parties as including transactions between "an enterprise and its principal owners or management" (paragraph 1). Accordingly, all transactions between Midwestern Lights or Northern Lights and any of the entities

---

[6] "Related Party Disclosures," *Statement of Financial Accounting Standards* No.57 (Stamford, Conn.: FASB, March 1982).

owned or controlled by Thomas Burns (e.g. Flying Sly, MTC, Ltd., and the Crimson Rose restaurant) should be considered related party transactions. The substance of such transactions should be examined carefully since the requisite conditions of competitive, free-market dealings do not exist (paragraph 15) and one party has an advantage over the other and can manipulate the terms of the transaction. Statement of Financial Accounting Standard No. 57 requires that the following disclosures be made with respect to related party transactions (see paragraph 2):

- The nature of the relationship involved.
- A description of the related party transactions.
- The dollar amounts of the related party transactions.
- Amounts due from or to related parties.

In his review of the books and records of Midwestern Lights and Northern Lights, Senior Investigator Bill Benson found evidence demonstrating lack of compliance with the above requirements.

All of the economic entity assumption violations discussed in Part 1 involved related party transactions. Accordingly, in my opinion, each of them can also be considered violations of SFAS No. 57 since the required disclosure information was not provided.

2. Basic Accounting Equation Violations

Assets are the resources owned by a business. Liabilities are the existing debts and obligations of a business. Owner's equity represents the ownership claims on total assets. The most fundamental of all generally accepted accounting principles is that the relationship of assets, liabilities, and owner's equity can be expressed by the following equation:

$$\text{Assets} = \text{Liabilities} + \text{Owner's Equity}$$

The Balance Sheet is a financial statement that reports the assets, liabilities, and owner's equity of a business at a particular date. Total assets must equal total liabilities and owner's equity. If all financial transactions occurring during a given period are recorded properly by the accounting personnel, the balance sheet should "balance;" that is, total assets should equal total liabilities and owner's equity. That a balance sheet should "balance" is an extremely basic principle of accounting. On behalf of both Midwestern Lights and Northern Lights, Thomas Burns entered into an agreement with MTC, Ltd. – wholly owned and managed by Thomas Burns – to manage both restaurants. Consequently, MTC personnel (e.g. Rochelle Bowman and Vivian Bowman) were responsible for the accounting systems for both Midwestern Lights and Northern Lights. The following investigative findings constitute basic accounting equation violations:

a.   *Midwestern Lights Balance Sheets Do Not Balance*

The Balance Sheets for Midwestern Lights (Midwestern Lights) do not balance for four accounting periods during 1997, and one during 1998. Specifically, Total Assets are less than Total Liabilities and Partnership Equity for the following periods:

Accounting Period	Amount of Discrepancy
4/30/97	$36,021.63
5/30/97	$37,580.26
6/30/97	$35,937.78
9/30/97	$17,215.75
3/31/98	$13,207.02

The fact that the Balance Sheets for Midwestern Lights do not balance for five accounting periods indicates that: (1) the MTC personnel do not possess the requisite knowledge and skills to competently record and report accounting information, and/or (2) the out-of-balance conditions are the result of employee/management defalcations or impropriety.

b.   *$44,000 Wire Transfer to U.S. Checking*

On July 16, 1997 $23,271.12 of Midwestern Lights cash funds were used to pay off a personal line of credit (i.e. State Bank loan number 451584) in the name of Thomas Burns. The withdrawal can be found on the July 1997 bank statement from State Bank. However, no entry is made in the accounting records to reduce the cash balance by $23,271.12. Consequently, the cash balance per books was falsely stated as being more than the cash balance per the bank statement. This violation of generally accepted accounting practice caused the accounting equation to be "out-of-balance."

The purpose of the overstatement in the cash account balance was to "cover up" the fact that $109,000 of Midwestern Lights investors' funds had been wire transferred to benefit the construction of Thomas Burns' restaurant in Trenton, Indiana. Since the financial activities of Midwestern Lights should be kept separate from the personal financial activities of Thomas Burns, this violates the economic entity assumption. Accordingly, any Midwestern Lights funds used to pay for the construction of Thomas Burns's restaurant in Trenton, Indiana constitutes a misappropriation of partnership assets.

This GAAP violation violates Section 4.3, Part (iii) of the Partnership Agreement, which specifically prohibits "any assets of the Partnership to become commingled with the assets of the General Partner as Manager."

c. *Errors in the Accounting Records*

The Benson report lists 61 different errors and/or irregularities in the accounting records of both Midwestern Lights and Northern Lights including things such as:

- Account category amounts not adding up to the general category totals.
- Accounts in the inventory section of the balance sheet being left off one month and then reappearing in later months.
- Ledger balances maintained by MTC do not equal the amounts reported on the Balance Sheet.
- Ending cash balances for one month do not equal the beginning cash balances for the next month.
- Accounting entries made without any supporting documentation.

In my opinion, the existence of so many errors and/or irregularities in the accounting records indicates that: (1) the MTC personnel do not possess the requisite knowledge and skills to competently record and report accounting information, and/or (2) the accounting errors and/or irregularities are the result of employee/management defalcations or impropriety.

1. Breaches of Fiduciary Duty[7]

Persons in a position of trust or fiduciary relationship, such as officers, directors, high-level employees of a business, owe certain duties imposed by law to their principals or employers. The principal fiduciary duties are loyalty and care.

Duty of loyalty. Requires that the employee/agent act solely in the best interest of the employer/principal, free of any self-dealing, conflicts of interest, or other abuse of the principal for personal advantage. Thus, corporate directors, officers, and employees are barred from using business property or assets for their personal pursuits.

Duty of care. A corporate officer, director, or high-level employee must conduct business affairs prudently with the skill and attention normally exercised by persons in similar positions. Fiduciaries who act carelessly or recklessly are responsible for any resulting loss to the business shareholders or other principals.

Thomas Burns, as the general partner responsible for managing both the Midwestern Lights and Northern Lights franchises, owed a fiduciary duty to the limited partners who invested money in the franchises. In my opinion, the following investigative findings constitute breaches of fiduciary duty owed by Thomas Burns to the limited partners.

---

[7] Source of information: *Fraud Examiners Manual*, Third Edition (2000). The Association of Certified Fraud Examiners. Austin, Texas.

a. *Franchise Options—Northern Lights*

Thomas Burns failed to apprise the Northern Lights limited partners of the cost and time sensitivity of the franchise options purchased by Northern Lights through Flying Sly. Consequently, franchise options costing $30,000 were either allowed to expire or were improperly transferred. Such acts constitute breaches of the fiduciary duties of care and loyalty owed by Thomas Burns to the limited partners of Northern Lights.

This failure violates Section 4.3, Part (iii) of the Partnership Agreement, which specifically prohibits "any assets of the Partnership to become commingled with the assets of the General Partner as Manager." In addition, it violates Section 10.3, Part (b) which prohibits the General Partner from "sell(ing) or otherwise dispos(ing) of Partnership property without first obtaining the approval of at least fifty-one percent (51%) in aggregate investment interest of the Limited Partners," and Part (c) which prohibits the General Partner from "possess(ing) Partnership property or assign(ing) its rights in specific Partnership property for other than a Partnership purpose."

b. *General Partner 1% Contributions*

Flying Sly, Inc. - wholly-owned by Thomas Burns - failed to make the required initial 1% General Partner capital contributions on a timely basis as required by law in connection with both the Northern Lights and Midwestern Lights franchises. Flying Sly, Inc. made its "contribution" using funds to which it was not entitled. Such an act constitutes a breach of the fiduciary duty of loyalty owed by Thomas Burns to the limited partners of both Northern Lights and Midwestern Lights.

This breach violates Section 6.1of the Partnership Agreement, which states that "the General Partner will make an initial Capital Contribution in cash in an amount equal to one percent (1%) of the aggregate Capital Contributions of the Partners on the date this Amended Certificate and Agreement of Limited Partnership is filed as required by law."

In addition, Thomas Burns and Rochelle Bowman presented Lee Otteson, a limited partner of both Midwestern Lights and Northern Lights, with a false document in an effort to establish that Burns had made his 1% General Partner capital contribution in Midwestern Lights. Such an act clearly constitutes a premeditated effort to deceive the limited partners and a breach of the fiduciary duty of loyalty owed by Thomas Burns to the limited partners of both Northern Lights and Midwestern Lights.

c.   MTC, Ltd. Management Agreement

Thomas Burns, as President of Flying Sly, entered into a Management Agreement with his wholly-owned corporation MTC, Ltd. to manage the Garnett Rose restaurant (Northern Lights). The agreement was not made at "arms length"[8] and grants MTC, Ltd. expenses in excess of the 5% management fee as set forth in the management agreement. Such an act constitutes a breach of the fiduciary duty of loyalty owed by Thomas Burns to the limited partners of Northern Lights.

This breach violates Section 4.2, Part (h) of the Partnership Agreement, which requires the General Partner "to engage accountants…and any and all other agents and assistants…and to compensate them in such reasonable degree and manner as may be necessary or advisable."

d. $100,000 Flying Sly Loan - Midwestern Lights / False Entries

To further disguise the fact that $109,000 of Midwestern Lights investor funds had been diverted to finance the construction of another restaurant being built by Thomas Burns in Trenton, Rochelle Bowman "created a false and misleading summary for activity in the Flying Sly account" which corroborates an alleged loan from Flying Sly to Midwestern Lights. However, no loan agreement or any other documentation has been found which corroborates the existence of the alleged loan. Rochelle Bowman later claimed that $100,000 represented a "loan from Flying Sly to the Trenton Domestic Beef" that was partially paid back. At least four deposits cited by Rochelle Bowman as being loan repayments from the Domestic Beef were in fact received from sources other than the Domestic Beef. Rochelle Bowman's own accounting for the alleged loan indicates that $44,202.39 was never paid back. Such efforts by Rochelle Bowman to conceal from Midwestern Lights investors the $109,000 unauthorized transfer of Midwestern Lights funds clearly constitute a premeditated effort to deceive the limited partners and a breach of the fiduciary duty of loyalty owed by both Rochelle Bowman and Thomas Burns to the limited partners of Midwestern Lights.

These efforts violate Section 4.3, Part (iii) of the Partnership Agreement, which specifically prohibits "any assets of the Partnership to become commingled with the assets of the General Partner as Manager." In addition, it violates Section 4.3, Part (ii) of the Partnership Agreement, which specifically prohibits the lending of "any assets of the Partnership to or guarantee any obligations of the General Partner, as Manager."

---

[8] An "arm's-length" transaction is one in which competitive, free market conditions exist (see SFAS No. 57, paragraph 3). Accordingly, for the agreement between MTC and MWI/CWI to be considered "arm's length" it should have similar terms and fees to competing property management companies.

e. *$51,418.49 Pay to MTC – Midwestern Lights / False Entry*
The November 1997 Midwestern Lights General Ledger includes an entry whereby $51,418.49 is debited to "Payable to MTC" and credited to "U.S. Checking." However, no documentation exists to corroborate this entry nor do any payments from the "U.S. Checking" account correspond with this entry. Accordingly, the entry is completely false as no payment was made to MTC. Such an act constitutes a breach of the fiduciary duty of care owed by Thomas Burns to the limited partners of Midwestern Lights.

f. *Winnipeg (Midwestern Lights) Rent Guarantee*
Thomas Burns received ten times the rent guarantee to which he was entitled. According to the partnership agreement, Thomas Burns was entitled to receive $960 under the rent guarantee, not the $9,600 he actually received. Such an act constitutes a breach of the fiduciary duty of loyalty owed by Thomas Burns to the limited partners of Midwestern Lights.

g. *Northern Lights Girls Calendar*
All activities associated with the development and distribution of the Northern Lights Girls Calendars constitute breaches of the fiduciary duties of loyalty and care owed by Thomas Burns to the limited partners of both Northern Lights and Midwestern Lights. The fiduciary duty of care was violated since the creation of the calendar constituted a breach of the Restaurants of America franchise agreement, thus exposing the limited partners to possible litigation by Restaurants of America. Ultimately, the calendars – whose creation had been financed by Northern Lights and Midwestern Lights – were transferred to Flying Sly without reimbursing Northern Lights and Midwestern Lights for the costs of creating the calendars. Such an act constitutes a breach of the fiduciary duty of loyalty owed by Thomas Burns to the limited partners of both Northern Lights and Midwestern Lights.

These breaches violate Section 4.3, Part (iii) of the Partnership Agreement, which specifically prohibits "any assets of the Partnership to become commingled with the assets of the General Partner as Manager." In addition, such activity violates Section 10.3, Part (b) which prohibits the General Partner from "sell(ing) or otherwise disposing of Partnership property without first obtaining the approval of at least fifty-one percent (51%) in aggregate investment interest of the Limited Partners," and Part (c) which prohibits the General Partner from "possess(ing) Partnership property or assign(ing) its rights in specific Partnership property for other than a Partnership purpose."

Summary Opinion

The Association of Certified Fraud Examiners defines fraud as follows:

> "Fraud includes an intentional or deliberate act to deprive another of property or money by guile, deception or other unfair means."

In my opinion, which is based on a reasonable degree of academic and professional certainty, in an effort to deprive the Limited Partners "of property or money by guile, deception or other unfair means," Thomas Burns, et al., deliberately and intentionally, violated numerous generally accepted accounting principles, violated numerous provisions of the Partnership Agreements, violated state securities laws, misappropriated partnership assets, and breached the fiduciary duties of care and loyalty he owed to the Limited Partners.

Submitted by:

Winston Woodruff
Winston Woodruff, Ph.D., CPA, CFE
Chief Executive Officer
Woodruff and Associates, LLP

Exhibit 2
Diagram of Parties Involved and Relationships in the
Thomas E. Burns Case

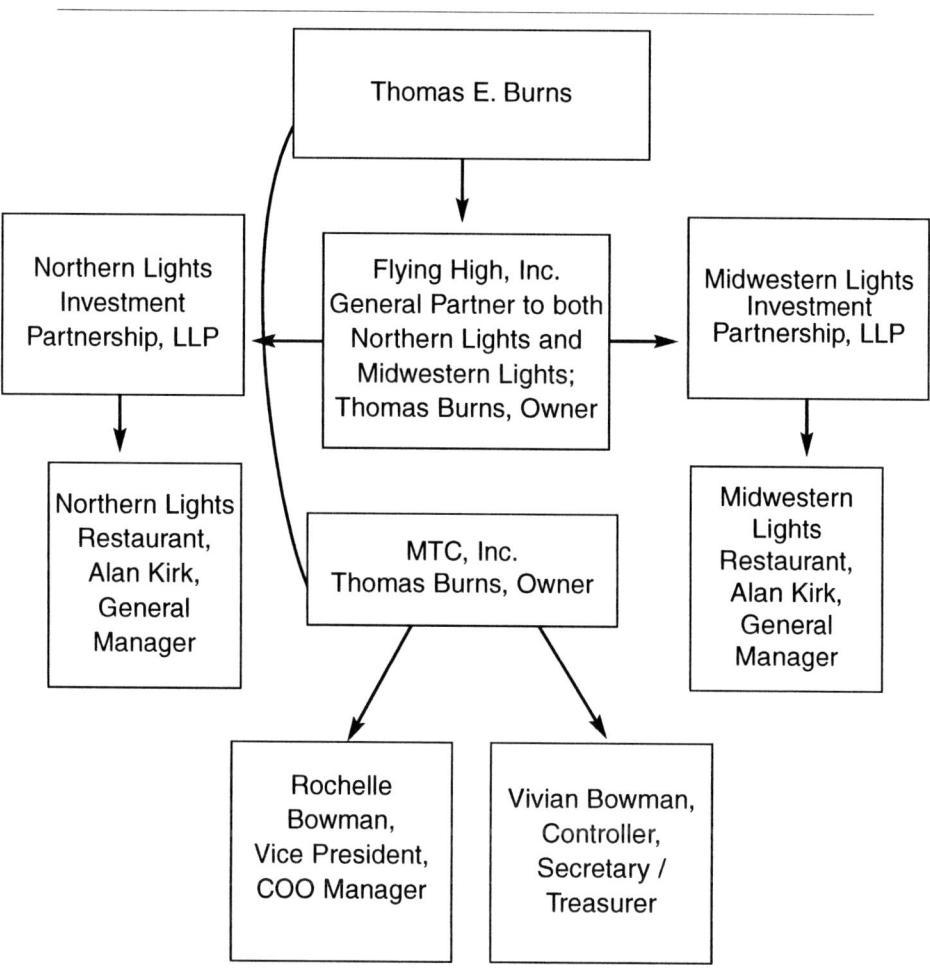

APPENDIX I

Factual Overview Prepared by Plaintiffs Attorneys

Players: The defendant in this dispute is Thomas E. Burns. Thomas Burns is the owner and president of MTC, Ltd., a restaurant management firm, which had been established over 25 years earlier. MTC is an important element of this case and served as the "enterprise" as required under the RICO[9] statute. Burns had hired two relatives, who were long-time associates of Burns to serve as other officers of MTC. Rochelle Bowman is Vice-president, and responsible for day-to-day operations; Vivian Bowman is Controller and Secretary/Treasurer. The Bowman sisters are co-defendants in this legal dispute. Burns and his co-defendants had used MTC to manage numerous restaurants in both the United States and Canada.

The plaintiffs in this dispute are majority interest investors in two limited partnerships, Northern Lights Investments (Northern Lights) and Midwestern Lights Investments (Midwestern Lights). Northern Lights and Midwestern Lights were formed to develop some vacant commercial property in the United States and Canada into two restaurant franchises. The Northern Lights and Midwestern Lights investors knew of Thomas Burns' restaurant management firm, MTC, Inc., and approached him about becoming a general partner in both Northern Lights and Midwestern Lights. Burns anticipated that the two restaurant franchises would be very successful, and in March 1998 Burns formed Flying Sly, Inc., a US business corporation solely to act as the General Partner in the Northern Lights and Midwestern Lights Limited Partnerships. Exhibit 2 graphically summarizes the relevant parties involved in this litigation.

Acting for Flying Sly as General Partner, Burns engaged his own corporation, MTC, Ltd. to manage the Franchise Restaurants owned by Northern Lights and Midwestern Lights. Each of the these limited partnership owns a 'Franchise' Restaurant; Northern Lights owns a Franchise Restaurant located in the United States and Midwestern Lights owns a Franchise Restaurant located in Canada.

The capitalization of Northern Lights was approximately US $1.0 Million cash from the limited partners. That capitalization served as the basis for calculating partner distributions. The capitalization of Midwestern Lights was approximately

---

[9] The Complaint makes a claim of a Racketeer Influenced Corrupt Organizations violation under Title 18 U.S. Code Section 1962(c) that states: It shall be unlawful for any person employed or associated with an enterprise engaged in, or the activities of which affect, interstate or foreign commerce, to conduct or participate, directly or indirectly, in the conduct of such enterprise's affairs through a pattern of racketeering activity or collection of unlawful debt.

US $0.75 Million cash from limited partners. The total amount entrusted to Thomas Burns, the General Partner for both Northern Lights and Midwestern Lights, was approximately US $1.75 Million.

Burns, as Flying Sly General Partner, engaged his corporation, MTC, Ltd. to manage the two Franchise Restaurants owned by Northern Lights and Midwestern Lights. Given the clear conflict of interest on Burns's behalf, the resulting contract was not arms-length. Notwithstanding, Rochelle Bowman and Vivian Bowman were responsible for the "bookkeeping" for the Franchise Restaurants. Neither of the Bowman sisters had any academic or professional training in accounting. Rochelle graduated from State University with a major in English and Vivian had some college education but no degree.

Specific Allegations of Fraud

Commingling of Funds. Defendant Burns, doing business as Flying Sly, Inc., together with the Bowman sisters, gained exclusive control over all partnership funds following initial deposit of the investment funds. Unbeknownst to the plaintiffs, Burns and the Bowman sisters immediately began diverting and commingling those funds with their separate non-partnership funds from other non-related restaurants and corporations which Thomas Burns and the Bowman sisters controlled. Using the Flying Sly account under his personal control, Burns then improperly commingled corporate and personal funds with partnership funds which continued until a majority of the limited partners removed Burns as the General Partner of Northern Lights and Midwestern Lights on October 26, 2000. Subsequently, Burns further "borrowed" approximately US $300,000 in partnership funds that he transferred to a non-partnership restaurant called Domestic Beef.

"Bootleg" Calendars. Burns had hired defendant Alan Kirk to act as regional manager of both Franchise Restaurants. While serving in that managerial position, Kirk, with instructions and the knowledge of Burns and Rochelle Bowman, began creating unauthorized swimsuit, pin-up-type calendars utilizing the financial resources of both Franchise Restaurants and featuring some of the restaurant employees. Since the franchisor created and sold similar calendars through franchisees, such calendars violated the franchise agreement. That agreement specifically prohibited franchisees from creating and selling calendars that compete with the franchisor's own products. The evidence further indicates that monies of both Franchise Restaurants were used to front the expenses of calendar production and were also used to sell the calendars. Further, rather than maintain the proceeds

from calendar sales of nearly US $500,000 as part of the assets of the two restaurants; they were diverted to bank accounts controlled exclusively by Thomas Burns.

Plaintiff's Investigation

The evidence supporting the Plaintiff's claims developed from an ongoing forensic accounting inquiry beginning in December 2000, and conducted by certified fraud examiners through Woodruff & Associates, LLP whose examiners include lead examiner Winston Woodruff, and Bill Benson. Exhibit A contains a copy of Plaintiff's expert Winston Woodruff's report of accounting irregularities.

Specific allegations of wrongdoing by Thomas Burns include securities law irregularities, commingling of limited partnership funds with Burns's personal funds, and various allegations of fraud. The foundation for all of the fraud allegations is the fiduciary duty, including duties of loyalty and care, owed by General Partner Thomas Burns to the limited partners of Northern Lights and Midwestern Lights. Hallmarks of the multi-tiered, complex scheme to defraud are categorized in over 20 areas of intentionally deceptive accounting practices, commingling and unlawful use of limited partnership funds, various cover-up tactics (including false statements to the limited partners), false entries in the books and records of the partnerships, and misappropriation of partnership funds into bank accounts controlled by Burns and his co-defendants.

Forensic accounting experts organized and reviewed over 28,000 documents. Expert Winston Woodruff asserts that the books and records of the limited partnerships' two Franchise Restaurants (i.e., Northern Lights and Midwestern Lights) were intentionally manipulated to facilitate and conceal the fraudulent schemes being perpetrated by Burns and his co-defendants. A non-exhaustive description of some 20 "badges" of fraud developed by certified fraud examiner Bill Benson are set out in a report which serves as the foundation for Woodruff's report.

Plaintiff's Damages

The Plaintiffs contend that direct economic damages totaling US $1.3 Million resulted from the Defendants wrongful acts and omissions. As of May 1, 2002, Plaintiffs have incurred or paid to the forensic accounting firm of Woodruff & Associates, LLP, approximately $175,000 for its services. Additionally, Plaintiffs have incurred or paid approximately $250,000 to legal counsel for services rendered in this matter. Thus, Plaintiff seeks $1.725 Million in damages, which if a RICO claim is proved will be trebled according to law.

APPENDIX II

Suggestions to Academics for using the Case as an Instructional Tool

As noted in the text of this case study, the contents are based on an actual case. Accordingly, the content is useful as an instructional tool in forensic accounting classes. For example, we use the case to illustrate (1) the complexities that surround real world cases, diagramming the important relationships in a real world case as an aid to understanding, (3) the importance of the expert witness report, and (4) preparation/analysis of the expert witness report. Accordingly, we suggest the following as an assignment, in whole or in parts.

Instructions to students:

1. Read pages 1 to 9 of the case, and the information in the Fraud Examiners Manual (or other material provided by instructor) on Expert Witness Reports.
2. Based on the information found in the section "A Case Study of Legal Dispute", prepare a chart depicting the important relationships discussed in the section.
3. Prepare a Factual Overview of the Case to be used by Plaintiff's Attorney's as an overview of the major points of background and findings for the court (instructors see Appendix I).
4. Analyze the Expert Report in light of suggestions of the ACFE, and by discussion which parts of the report are apparently the most difficult to construct and require the most judgment, those that are rudimentary, and feel free to include suggestions for changing the report.
5. This case, like most was actually settled out of court. Discuss reasons why the majority of cases settled out of court.

The instructor could assign all or part of these and/or additional instructions to be prepared in groups. Further, the instructor might assign a group to shoot holes, as it were, in the case prepared by the plaintiff.

CHAPTER 8

Note to Counsel: Timing is Important in Selecting an Expert Witness

Peter H. Burgher

A prominent southeastern Michigan law firm specializing in certain types of litigation recently asked me if I was able to serve as an expert regarding measurement of damages in an employee discharge case. As the lawyer, who was handling the matter for the partner in charge, explained during his initial phone call, the matter had proceeded through discovery and mediation was imminent. Following the normal course of timing after mediation, trial was just around the corner. The associate with whom I was working, primarily because the partner was tied up in several other matters at the time, presented me with a series of conclusions and asked whether I would have any trouble testifying as to these conclusions should the matter actually come to trial. The mediation summary had been prepared.

As I read through the pleadings and discovery testimony and reviewed the company's records regarding the employee's complaint of age discrimination, I raised a number of questions that occurred to me and asked counsel why they had not been addressed during deposition. Unfortunately, it turned out that these questions had not occurred to counsel. Then, in support of the research necessary to determine whether I could testify as requested I prepared a series of schedules regarding the plaintiff's poten-

Peter H. Burgher, CPA, is a retired managing partner at Arthur Young & Company, and has appeared as an expert witness on professional matters, damage measurement, lost profits, securities, fraud, and accounting issues. This chapter is reprinted with permission from *Lawyers Weekly USA*, the national newspaper for small-firm lawyers. You can get a free three issue trial subscription to *Lawyers Weekly USA* by visiting www.lawyersweeklyusa.com or calling 800-451-9998.

tial damages should the question of liability be decided in his favor. Plaintiff's complaint had some astronomical numbers for which there was no basis. Notwithstanding the lack of support for plaintiff's contentions, the schedules that I prepared even on the most conservative assumptions produced some astonishingly high numbers. Now the matter had gotten to the partner level and serious attention was being devoted. Client and counsel were quite anxious that my schedules not become known during the progression of the case. Of course, they were protected work product, but the concern was nonetheless well founded for the fact remained that if I was able to make such computations plaintiff might have an expert who could do so as well.

IMPORTANCE OF TIMING FOR LAWYERS

Obviously, the choice of an expert is one to be addressed very carefully. Notwithstanding which expert counsel chooses, the lesson from the above scenario was that timing was very poorly done. Had counsel engaged me or another expert earlier in the case before depositions were taken of plaintiff and his witnesses, they may very well have asked questions that could have had a material effect on the outcome of the case. Now that discovery was complete those questions could not be asked until the trial. The best defense is, of course, to prevent cases from going to trial when you are the defendant. Also, had the counsel the benefit of my computations before the matter got as far as mediation, they may have taken an entirely different strategic approach from simply attempting to stonewall the case and come to me with conclusions. All in all, the situation proved to be somewhat difficult and the outcome was a settlement far in excess of what might have otherwise been obtained had the case been managed more skillfully. At least, I was able to show them real exposure could have existed at trial.

Timing of the Expert's Work

In my experience, an expert, such as myself in the field of accounting, or in any other field of professional technology, will seldom cost more if he is engaged early on in a proceeding as compared with waiting until just before trial is ready to commence.

Usually, I have to do the same amount of work to prepare for testimony when I am engaged early on as compared when I am engaged late in the case. Sometimes, if I am engaged too late my time will be significantly more because of the need to find defenses and strategies that are "catch-up" in nature rather than being well planned in advance and addressed to the needs of the case. In other words, it sometimes costs more to repair damage than it does to prevent it through anticipation and careful homework.

The use of an expert to assist counsel in formulating questions for depositions, items and facts to be obtained during discovery, documents to be search for, and interrogatory guidance often proves to enhance substantially counsel's effectiveness in carrying out a good litigation strategy. Considering these areas in which an expert may be able to make a positive contribution should give you ideas as to haw they may apply to cases you are presently working on.

Experts need not be advocates to suggest to counsel ways in which their case strategy may be improved. Often, the expert has an insight into the case or the technology upon which the matter rests that is different from counsel's experience. Usually the expert' background and experience is far different from that of the client.

One exception in this regard applies when I am called to testify on matters relating to professional malpractice. In this type of case, the expert is very often a peer of counsel's client and their backgrounds and viewpoints may often be very similar. However, this exception need not invalidate the general rule that an expert, if he is skilled in his profession and experienced in court work, can bring an entirely new dimension to litigation that neither counsel nor the client can anticipate. In fact, that is often why experts are needed.

Further, sessions in which counsel, the expert and the client play "what if" are often very valuable in exploring avenues which may be anticipated or dealt with well before case strategy and trial script are ready to be committed. Every litigator has his own style for case management and such trial techniques as document retention and recovery, evidence organization, trial manners and the like, but these should have no impact on questions of strategy, matters of fact and, very importantly, the expert's opinion and what he is willing and prepared to testify to at trial.

Other Possible Outcomes

In one matter in which I was involved regarding a claim of lost profits, plaintiff had prepared an elaborate presentation of forecasts purporting to show what he would have earned had the business gone forward upon which the lost profits claim was based. Because I was engaged early in the development of the case, I had an opportunity to carefully study plaintiff's expert presentations and plaintiff's counsel pleadings.

Fortunately for my client, plaintiff's assumptions had several serious flaws and the presentation made by their experts was based upon an approach, which was entirely unproven and heretical. As luck would have it, plaintiff's counsel wanted very much to depose me as defendant's expert early on in the proceedings. My testimony demolished their case as it stood at the time and they were forced to redo their entire assumptions and presentations.

A lenient court allowed this and when they came to trial they were really unprepared and on very weak ground. As a consequence of their being forced to re-develop their case before trial, they did not handle the case very well and the result was an extremely favorable result for our client. Needless to say, counsel did an excellent job in taking full advantage of the situation

CAN EVERY EXPERT DO THIS?

Not at all! But, the likelihood is that your expert will be able to attack the other side's case much more effectively if he has the opportunity to do so early on in the game than if the case is fully developed before he has a chance to get at it. You can't always count on demolishing the other side's case just before they go to trial, but if you are well prepared and have plenty of time to develop your strategy, it is much more likely.

In another matter, in which a very careful and enlightened counsel was defending a professional malpractice case, we found that the other side had in fact "set up" the case from the very beginning and actions taken by the opponent had been calculated to put the defendant of the malpractice claim into a position where malpractice could be claimed. How did we discover this? We got into areas well aside from the ostensible initial reason for having an expert. But, because we had time to develop this theme we were able to ask the right questions, seek the right documents, and long before trial commenced to mount a series of proofs, which were inescapable.

CONSIDERATIONS IN CHOOSING AN EXPERT

Choosing an expert is not an easy task. There are several things which counsel should look for.

- First, counsel should look for an expert that has experience in his field. I don't mean just a little bit of experience, I mean a lot of experience. All too often persons are called to expertize on matters upon which they have peripheral knowledge, but unless they have practiced at some length in the area in which their testimony is going to be required, they may overlook items which will become important later on.

- Second, counsel should be careful to select an expert that is "court-wise." This means that your expert should have had trial experience and many cases under his belt before you place your case in his hands. How does an expert obtain this type of experience? The only way to get it is to be expertizing for a considerable length of time.
    That does not necessarily mean that the expert who has been holding himself out for twenty years is a better expert than the one who's been at it for ten years. What it means is counsel should look for the expert that has had the moist significant and relevant experience during the period of time he has been expertizing. Two hundred cases within a ten-year period is worth more than a hundred cases over twenty years.
    The expert should be aware of when to answer the question and when to expand his answer. Most trial judges will allow experts to roam freely in a complete exposition of their subject. There are times, however, when a simple, direct, and limited answer is best. You want

to be assured that your expert knows when to "answer only the question" and when to answer the "the real question." Case and trial experience should give some clue as to the expert's understanding of these concepts, but you can only find out for sure by questioning him intensively yourself.

- Third, counsel should look for an expert that is interested in the broader aspects of trial law. Not to say that the expert is going to try the case, but counsel should be looking for an expert that is imaginative, has experience in developing strategies, has an inquiring mind and a willingness to use it and gets enjoyment and exhilaration out of the process in which he is being utilized. An expert that is bored, dull, or not interested in what he is doing will produce a bad result in court. If your case should get to a jury, your expert should be able to carry himself well and make a positive presentation.

- Fourth, before you get too far into strategy, planning, and the mechanics of the case itself you should (along with some of your partners or associates if that is possible) test your expert to see how well he withstands close scrutiny and intensive questioning. You should be looking for an expert that does not wither under intensive fire. To a great extent, this comes from experience, but it also comes from having the type of personality and demeanor that enables the expert to carry himself with confidence, assurance and authority. Juries, and your client, will listen and believe an expert who conveys his message effectively. In addition to testing the expert yourself, reference checking should be employed to find out how the expert has actually performed previously in courtroom situations. Many people, however good they may be technically, come unglued in a courtroom setting. This is the last thing you want to happen after having invested a lot of your time and your client's money in developing your expert's knowledge of the case. All too unfortunately, humans make judgments about other humans based upon initial appearances, impressions and personal prejudices. Therefore, a college professor who comes across as a tweedy, rambling and inoffensive should will be less likely to impress a jury than a mathematically precise well suited conservative individual.

  Sometimes, certain types of forensic specialists can appear in the uniform of their trade. I know one trial lawyer who has dressed his medical experts in white hospital coats, for example, as if the person giving testimony came directly from making rounds. Law enforcement people sometimes can dress in their uniform, although it is singularly inappropriate for a retired law enforcement person to wear a uniform which he is no longer entitled to wear. Engineers, accountants, actuaries and the like should be dressed in precise, conservative business suits. I always wear either a solid blue gabardine suit that is trimly tailored or a light gray pin stripe, similarly tailored, along with a maroon spotted necktie.

I have noticed that little things, even to the extent of a person wearing a striped shirt, can seemingly give a jury the wrong impression. Once, I observed a case being lost by an attorney who wore a shirt with a collar of a different color. The jury upon later interview felt they did not trust counsel on the other side, even though they could not identify why. My observation was he came across as a dandy. That is the last thing you want the impression of your expert to be.

Other Qualifications

- Fifth, pick your expert from among those who have a working knowledge of the law. If the expert has a thorough understanding of trial procedure, cut-off dates, the meaning of mediation, the importance of motions and the like, he will be much more effective in serving you and the client. The importance of agreeing to and meeting deadlines cannot be overemphasized. In checking references you will want to ask how timely are the expert's efforts on developing questions for counsel and the like. Is the expert always early for meetings and does he make it to court on time?

  Beware of the expert who wants to come to court, recite his little specialty and leave without regard for the panoply of the entire proceeding. Look out for the expert who takes only a very narrow view of his experience, duties and responsibilities. Skilled opposing counsel often can make a mockery of the expert's testimony if the expert is not acquainted with the entire case situation and prepared to handle anything that comes. Nonetheless, the broad gauged and experienced expert needs to know when to trip up his cross-examining questioner and when to buy time to think over or delay answering.

INTEREST IMPORTANT

- Sixth, your expert should be interested in the entire matter. Be aware of an expert who maintains only a narrow interest in his particular chosen technology. An expert who studies all the pleadings, reads and understands the motions, participates in some strategy sessions and above all else, is willing to sit through the entire trial if necessary will be far more effective. Very often subtleties in opposing counsel's presentations, the judge's rulings, the jury's reactions and the like make a great deal of difference in the outcome of a case. If your expert has a handle on these and discusses them understandably with you so there is mutual utilization of all the actions going on, he will be far more effective than one who does not.

UNDERSTANDING OF CASE LAW

It is also important that the expert have an understanding of case law relative to matters within his undertaking.

For example, I was recently involved in a condemnation proceeding where costs were awarded to the plaintiff and upon motion of opposing counsel, a hearing concerning experts' fees was conducted by the trial judge. I could see that the judge was headed in a certain direction. Unknown to counsel for either side, there had been a case recently in the involved state where time expended by an expert in coaching counsel (that is education or training counsel) was not awardable. The judge expressed a line of questioning which required quick thinking on my part to minimize the impact of this precedent. Had I not been aware of this prior law, I might very well have been trapped into answers that were inappropriate.

PRIOR CONTRARY TESTIMONY

Another factor counsel should evaluate in selecting an expert is whether there has been prior contrary testimony by the expert somewhere in his career. Nothing can be more harmful to your expert's position than if counsel for the other side is able to obtain information on previous testimony by the same expert that is inconsistent with the position being taken on the matter at hand. Generally, it is safe to inquire of your expert whether there has been any inconsistent testimony in his experience and what the circumstances were.

CONCLUSION

It is a safe generalization that the timing of the use of experts is greatly enhanced by bringing your specialist in at the earliest possible time during the development of a case. Selection of an expert should be a thoughtful and carefully undertaken process which includes a thorough examination of the expert's experience, credentials and references.

CHAPTER 9

Deposition Preparation Outline

Steven Babitsky and James J. Mangraviti, Jr

The *Deposition Preparation Outline* you will find on the next two pages is the intellectual property of SEAK, Inc. It is reprinted with permission.

SEAK, Inc. publishes books for experts of all specialties including *Cross-Examination: The Comprehensive Guide For Experts, Writing and Defending Your Expert Report, How to Excel During Depositions,* and *The Comprehensive Forensic Services Manual.*

The *Outline* is designed to be a quick reference guide for all experts preparing for depositions. To request a free laminated, color version of this outline, please e-mail your name and address to mail@seak.com.

We hope that you find the *Deposition Preparation Outline* to be a valuable resource.

Steve Babitsky, Esq., is the President of SEAK, Inc. He trains hundreds of experts every year. Attorney Babitsky is seminar leader for the Annual National Expert Witness and Litigation Conference.

James J. Mangraviti, Jr., Esq has trained hundreds of expert witnesses across the United States and Canada. He is a former trial lawyer with experience in defense and plaintiff personal injury law and insurance law.

TYPE OF DEPOSITION
A. Preservation of evidence
B. Discovery

HOUSEKEEPING DETAILS
A. Manner of dress
B. Where and when to report
C. Parking availability
D. Estimated time of deposition
E. Who will be present for deposition

COMPENSATION
A. Obtain fee in advance
B. Charge for preparation, travel, and out-of-pocket expenses
C. Charge for last-minute cancellations

STIPULATIONS
A. Do not agree to waive reading and signing

YOUR PREPARATION
A. Locate all records and tests you have reviewed
B. Organize your file for easy reference
C. Review your opinion and case weaknesses/strengths
D. Discuss case with client attorney
E. Try to get opposing counsel's style, techniques and theory of the case
F. Think about the difficult questions and issues
G. Know the timeline in the case

PREPARATION WITH COUNSEL
A. Types of questions opposing counsel will ask
B. Questions retaining counsel will ask
C. Review legal standards and "magic words"
D. Look at contents of your file
E. Discuss what to bring to deposition
F. Update on status of litigation
G. Review of opinions

IN DISCOVERY DEPOSITION COUNSEL'S GOALS ARE TO
A. Learn opinions
B. Explore qualifications
C. Lock down the expert
D. Evaluate credibility
E. Probe for bias
F. Learn factual assumptions
G. Gather as much information as possible
H. Use the expert to bolster counsel's case
I. Intimidate the expert
J. Learn as much as possible about the case

SUBPOENAS
A. Have you received a subpoena duces tecum?
B. Have you complied with the subpoena?

CURRICULUM VITAE
A. Make sure it is accurate and up-to-date
B. Bring extra copies to deposition
C. Any exaggerations?

INCONSISTENT PRIOR STATEMENTS
A. Interrogatories
B. Prior written statements and reports
C. Prior cases

INVOLVEMENT IN CASE
A. When were you first contacted concerning this case?
B. By whom were you contacted?
C. How were you contacted: phone, letter, e-mail, other?
D. When did you accept the case?

RELATIONSHIP WITH COUNSEL
A. What is your personal/financial relationship with counsel who has retained you in this case?

WORK YOU HAVE DONE IN THIS CASE
A. Records and documents reviewed: Which ones and when?
B. Examination: What was done and when was it done?
C. Testing: What was done, when was it done, and what were the results?
D. Is all of this work reflected on your bills and invoices?
E. What additional work do you anticipate doing prior to the trial?

EDUCATIONAL BACKGROUND
A. What schools have you attended?
B. What were your major areas of study?
C. What degrees did you obtain?
D. What are the dates for your attendance and degrees?
E. What additional training courses have you attended?
F. What continuing education courses have you attended in the past ten years?
G. Have you been the subject of any disciplinary actions?
H. Have your licenses ever been suspended or revoked?
I. What were your grades?
J. What did you do between any gaps in your education?

OPINIONS
A. The opinions you will be testifying to
B. The facts and assumptions upon which the opinions are based
C. The methodology employed in deriving the opinion
D. When the opinion was first formed
E. The documents you used in forming the opinion
F. The degree of flexibility in the opinion
G. How the proposed opinion compares to answers previously given during discovery

ORGANIZATIONS
A. What professional organizations and societies are you a member of?
B. What is your status in these organization(s)?
C. Have you ever paid a fee to obtain additional credentials?

FORENSIC INCOME
A. Percentage of income from forensic work
B. Percentage of time testifying for plaintiffs
C. Percentage of time testifying for defendants

PUBLICATIONS
A. State all of the articles, chapters, books, reviews, abstracts, and other writings that you have had published
B. When and where were these published?
C. Specify if any of your writings have not been accepted for publication

DATES
Make sure you know the key dates:
A. When you were first contacted by counsel
B. When you were retained as an expert
C. When you received the records
D. From whom they were received
E. When you formed your opinion(s) in the case
F. The date of the event in question
G. The date(s) key tests were performed

FEES
A. Hourly rate
B. Rate for deposition and trial testimony
C. Amount billed/paid to date
D. Future billing

WHAT MATERIALS OR RECORDS WERE YOU PROVIDED? BY WHOM? WHEN WERE THEY PROVIDED?

A. Correspondence
B. Reports
C. Messages
D. Notes
E. Computer disks/e-mails/files
F. Police reports
G. Investigative reports
H. Medical and hospital records
I. Literature
J. Tables
K. Standards
L. Contracts
M. Photographs
N. Videotapes
O. Research
P. Test results
Q. Other materials

VIDEOTAPE DEPOSITIONS

A. Prepare with counsel and practice before a videotape camera
B. Dress conservatively
C. Look directly at the camera when testifying
D. Avoid long pauses that may make you look evasive or uninformed
E. When handling exhibits, make sure you hold them so that they can be appreciated by the viewers
F. Avoid eating, smoking, drinking, chewing gum, or chewing on pens or pencils
G. Turn off pagers, cell phones, and beepers
H. Avoid making unnecessary and distracting noise by rustling papers, touching the microphone, or moving furniture
I. Avoid being goaded into flashes of anger, arrogance, and combativeness
J. Watch out for your nonverbal behavior and body language
K. Don't let counsel lead your eyes away from the camera

GENERAL ADVICE

A. Tell the truth
B. Act naturally
C. Don't be arrogant
D. Avoid slang
E. Be careful of what you highlight or write down
F. Don't argue with counsel
G. Don't elaborate
H. Don't estimate
I. Don't exaggerate
J. Don't guess
K. Don't interrupt the question
L. Don't lose your temper
M. Don't speculate
N. Leave yourself an out
O. Listen carefully to the questions
P. Make sure you know your role in the case
Q. Don't joke
R. Pause before answering
S. Read the documents before you testify about them
T. Say you don't know if you don't know
U. Say you don't remember if you don't remember
V. Stay within your area of expertise
W. Take breaks when needed
X. Avoid absolute and hedge words

PLEADINGS

A. Complaint
B. Answer
C. Interrogatories
D. Depositions
E. Motions
F. Motions to compel
G. Others

AUTHORITATIVE TEXTS

A. Know what is "authoritative"
B. Do not commit unless you see the text

BREAKS

A. Ask for breaks when needed
B. Don't consult with retaining counsel during breaks

ANSWERING DEPOSITION QUESTIONS

A. Tell the truth
B. Answer only what you are asked and do not volunteer information
C. Pause before answering
D. Actively listen to the entire question and do not interrupt
E. "I don't know" may be an appropriate response
F. Don't exaggerate, speculate, or guess
G. Keep your cool
H. Do not argue with counsel or get involved in the lawyers' arguments
I. Don't fall for the "silence" gambit
J. Avoid jokes, sarcasm, and inappropriate remarks
K. Don't ramble
L. Avoid absolute words
M. Be flexible and be prepared to concede some points
N. Avoid slang
O. Don't fall for the "bumble and fumble" gambit
P. Do not act like a jerk
Q. If confused, ask for the question to be repeated
R. Ask to see documents, reports, and statements before answering questions about them
S. Take adequate time to review any "new" documents, reports, etc.
T. Prepare thoroughly

DAUBERT ISSUES

A. Has the theory or technique used been tested?
B. Has the theory or technique been subjected to peer review and publication?
C. What is the known or potential rate of error of the method used?
D. What is the degree of the method's acceptance within the relevant scientific community?

CHAPTER 10

Cross-Examination:
The Comprehensive Guide for Experts

Steven Babitsky and James J. Mangraviti, Jr.

6.5 OPINIONS AND BASES FOR OPINIONS

The main reason expert testimony is presented is to offer an expert opinion. Accordingly, experts can anticipate being closely cross-examined on their opinions. They should also expect to be closely questioned on the bases of these opinions because an expert opinion is only as strong as the facts and reasoning upon which it is based. Questions in these areas are best blunted by carefully and honestly forming an opinion that is based on reliable methodology, a thorough investigation, and solid facts.

The specific areas an expert can expect questioning on are dealt with in the sections below. These include the following:

- The reliability of the expert's methodology used to formulate an opinion. This includes the factors dealing with reliability commonly addressed in *Daubert* challenges. For example, (1) whether the expert's theory can be or has been tested; (2) whether there is general acceptance of the expert's methodology within the relevant scientific community; (3) whether the methodology has been subjected to peer-reviewed publication; and (4) the known or potential error rate of the expert's methodology.

Steve Babitsky, Esq., is the President of SEAK, Inc. He trains hundreds of experts every year. James J. Mangraviti, Jr., Esq has trained hundreds of expert witnesses across the United States and Canada. This chapter is excerpted with permission from their book: *Cross-Examination: The Comprehensive Guide for Experts* © 2003 SEAK, Inc. ISBN: 1-892904-23-3.

- The factual assumptions upon which the expert opinion is based.

- Conflict between the expert's opinion and that of other, potentially more qualified, experts.

- Any underlining or notations made by the expert in the documents she used to formulate her opinion.

- Any information or records that the expert did not have available when forming her opinion. The cross-examiner will try to show that this information may have changed the expert's opinion.

- The parts of documents provided to the expert that she did not review. These may have contained important information that the expert failed to consider.

- The numbers, figures, and formulas used by the expert.

- Any passage of time between the incident in question and the expert's examination or inspection. Conditions or circumstances may have changed.

- The amount of time spent on the case. Did the expert pad his bill? Was there a rush to judgment?

- Reliance on other experts' opinions or reports. Can these be verified? Were they reliable?

- The degree of certainty the expert maintained when expressing his opinion or factual assumptions. Was it merely possible? Probable? How likely is it that the expert is mistaken?

- The standard of care the expert applied if this is a professional malpractice case. The expert cannot reliably testify as to the standard of care if she does not completely understand the standard of care as it applies in the jurisdiction in question.

Daubert/reliability of proposed testimony

Experts should be aware that their opinions are likely to be closely scrutinized under the *Daubert* doctrine to see if they are not only relevant but reliable.[1][1] Pursuant to the *Daubert* line of cases[2][2] and Federal Rule 702, the judge will act as a gatekeeper to screen out and exclude unreliable expert testimony and reports. The judge will consider several factors, including:

1. whether the theory or technique used by the expert can be, and has been, tested,

2. whether the theory or technique has been subjected to peer review and publication,

3. the known or potential rate of error of the method used, and

4. the degree of the method's or conclusion's acceptance within the relevant scientific community.

Procedurally, what will usually happen is that opposing counsel will make a motion in limine, which asks the judge to exclude the expert's testimony for failure to comply with the requirements of *Daubert* and Federal Rule of Evidence 702. The judge will then convene a hearing on the motion. At this "*Daubert*" hearing, the expert will be questioned closely (out of the jury's presence) on the issue of the reliability of his testimony.

Even if the judge allows the expert's testimony into evidence, questions regarding the reliability of the expert's opinion and methodology may still be allowed in front of the jury because these questions go to the weight to be given to the testimony. An expert opinion will survive *Daubert* challenges if the opinion is based upon reliable methodology and if the expert spells out this methodology clearly.

---

[1] [1] See *Daubert v. Merrell Dow Pharmaceuticals, Inc.*, 509 U.S. 579, 113 S.Ct.2786 125 L.E.2d 469 (1993); *General Electric Co. v. Joiner*, 522 U.S. 136, 118 S.Ct. 512, 517, 139 L.E.2d 508 (1977); and *Kumho Tire Co. Limited v. Carmichael*, 526 U.S. 137, 119 S.Ct. 1167, 143 L.E. 2d 238 (1999). See also Federal Rule of Evidence 702.

[2] [2] The Daubert approach to the admissibility of expert testimony applies in federal courts and many state courts.

The cross-examination the expert will likely face in *Daubert* hearings can be detailed, exhaustive, and very challenging. The following example involved a product liability action brought against the manufacturer of a lift truck. The expert opined in his report that powered fork positioners were available and widely used in 1991. An excerpt of the cross-examination of the expert on this issue follows.

Example 6.51: Expert cannot name any powered fork positioners that were available in 1991

Q. To your knowledge, does the Raymond Corporation design and manufacture a powered fork positioner?

A. (Pause.) Near as I can recall from Mr. Rogers' deposition, they did
   not.

Q. Would you agree then if they did not so design or manufacture a product, they would have to go out and get one on the open
   marketplace to supply for a truck like the model 40?

A. Yes.

Q. Are you aware of the existence of one or more manufacturers of powered fork positioners in the country or the world?

A. Yes.

Q. More than one?

A. think so.

Q. To your knowledge, are there different sizes, shapes, weights, and con-
   figurations of powered fork positioners that are available in the marketplace?

A. Sure.

Q. Are you prepared to identify for me the single type, model, design,
   configuration, size, weight, of powered fork positioner you contend
   the Raymond Corporation should have put on its Raymond model 40
   forklifts as standard equipment?

A. No.

Q. Why not?

A. Didn't think it was necessary. It's a feasible thing. I didn't think it was necessary to go into the details.

...

Q. You're not prepared to select which one or ones are available in the open marketplace or were available in the marketplace in 1991 when the subject Raymond model 40 was produced that would satisfy your engineering muster or your engineering test?

A. At this point, no. There is just no need. There was no question that it was feasible.

Q. Is there a single powered fork positioner that you can identify for me today that was available in 1991, which if installed on the Raymond model 40 forklift, you would say that truck is no longer defective in design?

A. Not a specific model, no.

Q. How about a manufacturer?

A. No.

Lesson: The preceding example was based upon the case of *Milanowicz v. The Raymond Corporation*, 148 F. Supp. 2d 525 (D. N.J. 2001). The court found that because the expert's testimony was unreliable, it was inadmissible. The court stated:

> Stephens also did not find adequate support for his conclusions in the relevant literature. While he claims to have reviewed a number of manuals and articles, the only citations he provides in his report are for the rather uncontroversial propositions that the elimination of identifiable, foreseeable hazards is a fundamental concern in industrial design and that users be warned of those hazards which have not been eliminated. (Pls.' Opp. Br. Ex. B at 7-8). As he testified at his deposition, he used these references as the "foundation" for his report. (Def.'s Supp. Br. At 235). However, he conceded that he [had] never seen a technical publication or any other document which criticized lift trucks such as the

Raymond Model 40 for not utilizing powered fork positioners were a necessary safety feature. (*Id.* at 184). In
short, beyond general design principles, Stephens identified nothing in the literature which would suggest
peer review of his conclusions.

The central contention of Stephen's report, and thus of
Plaintiff's case, is that, because powered fork positioners
were available and widely used in 1991, Raymond
should have incorporated this device into its Model 40
lift truck. (Pls.'s Opp. Br. Ex. B. at 8; Opp. Br. At 18).
Leaving aside Plaintiffs' mistaken contention that an
expert's experience is sufficient to satisfy Rule 702,
Stephens fails to adequately substantiate his contentions
that powered fork positioners were available and widely used in 1991. At 538.

Experts involved in this type of high-stakes litigation should be familiar
with *Daubert* and the cases that explain its holding. It's best to prepare
for intense scrutiny of one's expert report, deposition, and proposed trial
testimony. Retaining counsel should help the expert prepare for this
intensive cross-examination.

Example 6.52: No studies; investigation based on mere observation

Q. What do you mean when you say there is, quote, high potential for
contamination during fueling, closed quote?

A. Well, you've got to take your nozzle. It's got fuel under pressure behind
it. You've got to run it over the top of the step going in and coming
out. If you're a little lax or slow or just don't give a damn and you got
fuel pouring out of the nozzle as you're going in and out, you really got
a lot on the step.

Q. What studies have you made to determine whether the potential for
that is high or low or nonexistent?

A. I haven't done any studies.

Q. What investigation have you made?

A. Just normal observance of people and what they do when they fuel
vehicles.

Q. Now, tell us, please, what testing helps you conclude that there could have been a light coating of diesel fuel on the steps to the truck?

A. The application of diesel fuel to aluminum, the exposure of the aluminum for a number of days to reasonably comparable weather conditions.

Q. So, quote, this coating would have resulted from fuel spillage during fueling of the truck on Friday [the day of the accident], period, closed quote.

A. Yes.

Q. What is the basis for saying that the truck was fueled on Friday?

A. Well, there is no factual basis for that. Let's just say that we made an assumption that the truck was run on Friday. Maybe it was run on Saturday and that the truck was fueled up for the Sunday morning run…

Q. Did you conduct, as a part of your investigation, make any effort to determine why Mr. Fedor did not detect the diesel fuel on the step before he fell.

A. Good question. I don't know why he wouldn't have. You know, could be wind conditions. I don't know.

Q. Did you make any efforts to determine if there was any amount of diesel fuel on the step at the time that Mr. Fedor performed his required pretrip inspection why Mr. Fedor did not detect the diesel fuel on the step before he fell?

A. I have no idea.

Lesson: In the above example, the expert's testimony on the issue of design defect regarding the fuel port location was excluded at a motion in limine.

For additional information about the above example, see *Fedor v. Freightliner, Inc.*, 193 F.Supp.2d 820 (E.D. Pa. 2002).

Example 6.53: No testing, test results, prototypes, or publication on proposed alternative design

Q. As I understand it, sir, you offer two proposed failsafe designs for disposable butane cigarette lighters, correct?

A. Yes.

Q. According to you, a child's ability to operate the lighter would be made extremely difficult by your design?

A. Yes.

Q. Very difficult and failsafe are not the same thing, correct?

A. Yes. But it is extremely unlikely a child could operate the lighter.

Q. That's not failsafe, is it sir?

A. No.

Q. Have you tested your design to show it can be built?

A. No.

Q. Have you provided [a] drawing of the design?

A. No.

Q. Have you provided a design, prototype, or test results for your locking latch?

A. No.

Q. Have you developed or tested prototypes of lighters embodying your alternative designs or identified any product in the marketplace utilizing these designs?

A. No. It is not practical for a design expert like myself in a child's personal injury case to develop a working prototype of every design alternative to the product which I am proposing.

Q. So, your answer is no?

A. A prototype like you are suggesting would cost $20,000–$40,000 to build.

Q. So, your answer is no?

A. That's correct.

Q. Do you have any test results for your theory that your design would actually disable the lighter if the safety feature was removed?

A. No. I could not test something that does not exist.

Q. You stated earlier that your opinions were based on Bic's patents?

A. Yes.

Q. In fact, your opinions are based on your revisions, modifications, and adaptations to these patents, correct?

A. Yes. But these were only small and minor changes.

Q. Not unlike the minor modifications to an existing skywalk design made in the 1981 collapse of a skywalk in which 114 people were killed?

A. Counsel, I am not aware of the details of that 1981 accident.

Q. Have you written or published any articles describing your theories?

A. No.

Q. You would agree that you have not tested a prototype of your design, tested a product in the marketplace that embodies your design, or reviewed test results performed by others on your proposed designs?

A. That's true. But I still believe they would work.

Q. I am sure that you do.

Lesson: Prior to agreeing to testify in product liability cases, experts should attempt to make sure that their proposed testimony would meet the reliability standards of *Daubert*. The intense scrutiny their testimony is likely to bring means that additional testing, prototypes, or designs may be necessary to ensure the admissibility of the testimony. The expert should review these *Daubert* issues in depth with retaining counsel prior to accepting the assignment. A frank discussion of the financial resources of retaining counsel, his budget, and expectations is advisable as well.

The above example is based on the case of *Colon v. Bic USA, Inc.*, 2001 WL 1631402 (S.D. N.Y. 2001).

Factual assumptions

An expert's opinion is only as good as the factual assumptions upon which it is based. Experts should anticipate that they will be cross-examined on the assumptions upon which they based their opinion(s). The line of questioning by counsel will usually include:

- questions eliciting all the assumptions the expert used and
- questions about the accuracy or the validity of these assumptions.

Please consider the following example:

Example 6.54: Multiple assumptions of future events underlie opinion

Q. One of your assumptions, I assume, is that Mrs. Schaible would continue to want to work during all of those years as opposed to being a housewife and mother?

A. Yes, for the years after she would be age 42.

Q. And, of course, if for one reason or another she decided she didn't want to work that would affect your calculations, would it not?

A. That's correct.

Q. It is one of your assumptions that would continue throughout her working life?

A. Yes.

Q. Even after they got in their forties and fifties, your assumption was that she would still continue?

A. That's correct.

Q. She wouldn't keep any of her own earnings for herself [f]or whatever purpose, they would all go other than the 30 percent that you subtracted for the cost of her maintenance, one of your assumptions was that all of it would go to Mr. Schaible or at least he would receive the economic benefit of that?

A. I assumed beyond the 30 percent, right.

Q. One of your assumptions, I assume, was that the marriage would coninue during that period?

A. Yes. All the indications I had it was a happy marriage.

Q. But that was one of your assumptions?

A. Based on the information I have.

Q. And one of your assumptions, I assume, also was that Mr. Schaible would not remarry and everything would remain the same up to his own death?

A. Yes.

Q. Another one of your assumptions was that Mrs. Schaible would continue in good health and be able to work?

A. That's correct.

Q. Will you agree, Mr. Tansky, there is really no way you can say for sure any of the assumptions you made and upon which your opinions were based are valid with reference to this particular individual other than your opinion?

A. Could you restate that question?

Q. Okay, I can try, anyway. Would you agree there's really no way you can say, talking about you, now, for sure, that any or all of the assumptions that you have made and upon which your opinions are based, are valid, or would turn out to be valid with reference to this particular individual?

A. In my opinion?

Q. No, I'm not asking for your opinion, I'm asking whether there's any way you can say they will be valid.

A. No, things might have been better or worse economically.

Q. So, what we are saying, again, you don't have a crystal ball, you don't know what is going to happen in the future or what would happen with reference to any one specific individual?

A. That's correct.

Lesson: Counsel in the above example painstakingly went through the many assumptions the expert used to reach his conclusions and opinion. The expert appeared to be surprised and ill-prepared to discuss his assumptions. The expert did not reply artfully to the validity question and made no attempt to support his opinions. He could have replied to the last question: "Counsel, I based my assumptions and opinion on the facts. As such, they are valid and accurate. The reason we make assumptions based upon the facts is to as accurately as possible reach conclusions and opinions. I don't have a crystal ball. That is why factual, accurate assumptions are vital to reaching valid opinions."

This example is based upon the case of *Schaible v. Myers*, 311 N.W. 2d 297 (Mich. 1981). The court found the cross-examination was permissible and reasonable and explained:

> We conclude that the Court of Appeals erred. The jury was not told to take into account the possibility that the plaintiff might remarry. Rather it listened to an exposition of the many assumptions upon which the expert witness relied in making his calculations of the plaintiff's economic loss. Such an exposition is necessary to an intelligent understanding and evaluation of the worth of the expert's opinion. At 299.

Conflict with opinions of other experts

Cross-examining counsel may attempt to get an expert to change his opinion because it conflicts with one or more opposing experts' opinions. Counsel may take one of four approaches:

- Because two, three, four, or more different experts have different opinions, a "reasonable" expert would consider changing his opinion.

- Opposing experts are more qualified on this particular issue. For example, the other experts are specialists, thus a "reasonable" expert would defer to these opinions.

- The expert's opinion is out in left field because it stands in stark contrast to many experts, treatises, etc.

• The expert examined the plaintiff on only one occasion, but the examining physician saw him thirty-two times over a period of four years. Isn't she in a better position to opine about the plaintiff's condition?

Effective experts stick by their honest opinions and are prepared to justify why their opinions are just as valid, reliable, and worthy of acceptance as any others. Please consider the following examples.

Example 6.55: "Would another expert's different opinion change your opinion?"

Q. Doctor, if radiologists had read the same x-rays that you – and had a different opinion than you did, would that in any way change your opinion?

Ms. Keeley: Objection.

The Witness: I'm not certain why it should, because I had the opportunity to look at the x-rays myself.

…

Ms. Keeley: Objection, hearsay.

The Witness: You know, you're – you're creating a hypothetical situation and the answer is, is that in this particular case, I had the opportunity to review the x-rays. I sat down with all of them together which perhaps if the radiologists had reviewed them they didn't have the opportunity to look at all of them together. And there would be no reason for me to rely on somebody else's opinion when something's right in front of me.

Lesson: Experienced experts are not afraid to stand up for their opinions and point out why their opinions are just as valid, if not more valid, than those of opposing experts. In the above example, the expert stood his ground and gave a good explanation of why he might have been in the best position to offer an opinion.

For additional information about the above example, see *Daisey v. Keene Corporation*, 633 A.2d 979 (N.J. Super. A.D. 1993).

Example 6.56: None of the 5 other experts diagnosed malingering

Q. Now, Doctor, you've reviewed the medical records of Dr. Goff?

A. Yes.

Q. And he didn't make a diagnosis of malingering?

A. That's correct, he did not.

Q. Similarly with Dr. Finley?

A. That's correct.

Q. And, in fact, it was his opinion that she was not malingering?

A. That's right.

Q. Dr. Lord, he didn't make a diagnosis of malingering?

A. That's correct, he did not.

Q. And nor did Dr. Cherry, Dr. Manlove?

A. That's correct.

Q. None of the medical professionals, either physical medicine professionals or mental health professionals, have made a diagnosis of malingering other than yourself?

A. That's correct.

Q. So you would agree with me, you're the first medical professional engaged in this matter to make a diagnosis of malingering?

A. Yes, that is correct.

Q. And you've never physically examined her?

A. That's true.

Q. And you don't practice physical medicine?

A. No.

Q. And you're not suggesting that this injury, this admitted injury, didn't occur, are you?

A. No, I'm not suggesting that.

Lesson: Despite the contrary opinions of five other experts, the expert in the above example did not argue with counsel nor did he change his opinion. Note that counsel did not ask him why he thought he was correct and the other five experts were wrong.

Underlining in records and reports

Experts generally base their opinions to a large degree on documents that they have reviewed. Experts who note, highlight, or underline records or reports should expect to be cross-examined about their actions. Counsel will ask them why they selected a few specific sections to underline or highlight. To avoid this type of cross-examination, experts are well-advised to refrain from marking the documents upon which their opinion is based. It may be better practice to make notations on removable paper tags.

Example 6.57: "Why did you choose that phrase and underline it in red?"

Q. The attorney tells you that and states an opinion that the MRI showed evidence of disc protrusion. Correct?

A. Yes, sir. He again; I'm not here to defend the attorney, what I'm simply saying is what the attorney's letter is, is a summary of the medical records which include the diagnosis rendered by other physicians.

Q. He also mentions on the first page of his report that his client's tires had spikes in them that he believes were laid down by the picketers. Do you see that in the first page of his four-page letter to you?

A. Yes, sir.

Q. Why is it important for him to include that information to you? Do you know why?

A. You'd have to ask him, sir. I don't....

Q. Do you think that was important in coming up with your opinions and conclusions?

A. I don't think it was relevant at all, sir.

Q. Then why did you underline it in red on the letter that is contained in your file?

A. Why did I underline it in red?

Q. Right there you underlined that particular phrase in red right at the bottom of that first page.

A. Probably went through here and underlined various articles in there as I wrote it.

Q. I'm trying to figure out why you picked that one phrase on the one page and underlined it in red.

A. I can't tell you why, sir. I did it at the time I did it. Maybe I thought it was an interesting observation. So as I read through his letter, I underlined various things. I cannot give you the exact thought process why I did it, sir.

Lesson: Experts are better served when they do not underline, highlight, mark, or otherwise annotate documents that they review. If an expert realizes that this was done previously in the case, she should prepare for the inevitable questions during cross-examination. This expert gave a believable answer, namely, "I can't tell you why, sir ... Maybe I thought it was an interesting observation."

Missing records

It is common for retaining counsel to not provide an expert with all of the relevant documents in a case. Unfortunately, experts who do not review all the records in a case or who do not have access to them can expect to be cross-examined closely on this issue. Counsel will try to show directly, or by implication, that because the expert did not have all the facts, the assumptions on which she based her opinions are incomplete or flat out wrong. The more records that were not reviewed, the more suspect the expert's opinion. To avoid this type of cross-examination, experts should insist that retaining counsel provide them with all relevant documents. Please consider the following example.

Example 6.58: Expert has not reviewed many records

Q. Dr. Rungee, have you reviewed the records of Dr. Garvin and Dr. Seshul at Baptist Hospital?

A. I have not.

Q. Okay. Have you reviewed the records of Baptist Care Center as they relate to Mr. Clifford Charles Leverette?

A. I have not.

Q. Have you reviewed the records of HealthSouth, Dr. Richard Lisella, and Tammy Morton, PT, as they relate to Clifford Charles Leverette?

A. No, I have not.

Q. Have you reviewed the records as they relate to Mr. Clifford Charles Leverette of the Bedford County Medical Center, Dr. Ilarde, Knoblach, Galvez, Clark, and Tamula?

A. I have not.

Q. Have you reviewed the records of Dr. Thomas Woolridge as they relate to Mr. Clifford Charles Leverette?

A. I don't remember all these names.

Q. I didn't see it in there earlier.

A. No, I have not.

Q. Okay. Did you review the records of the Williamson Medical Center as they relate to Mr. Clifford Charles Leverette?

A. Who would be the physician?

Q. Doctors Metzman, McNamara, and Himmelfarb.

A. No.

Q. What about the records of Nashville Diagnostic Imaging, Dr. William Witt?

A. Is that his myelogram?

Q. It's an MRI. Here it is. It's this one. Have you seen that?

A. I have not.

Lesson: The expert who does not have access to all relevant case materials and has not reviewed them is at a serious disadvantage during cross-examination. Because he has not seen the records, he cannot honestly testify as to how the records would affect his assumptions and opinions. Experts are much better served by insisting on receiving all the records before they render an opinion. Where certain information was not reviewed, this should be honestly acknowledged, as above.

Only "relevant" or "pertinent parts" of records reviewed

When an expert is provided with or simply chooses to review selected portions of the record, he becomes vulnerable to cross-examination. An opinion based on incomplete or erroneous assumptions can easily be shown to be suspect. To blunt such challenges, experts should insist on reviewing as much information as is reasonably feasible. Please consider the following examples:

Example 6.59: Counsel did not send over all the records

Q. Your opinion is that the shooting was foreseeable due to the inadequate training of the security officers, correct?

A. Yes.

Q. As you did not perform an investigation, your opinion was based on the documents you reviewed?

A. Yes, that plus my education, training, and experience.

Q. You reviewed relevant portions of the:
    a. depositions of Ann Jefferson, Tom Davis, and Ray Ellis
    b. complaint
    c. answer
    d. incident report #69-107-12 dated 4/6/98
    e. the public safety services agreement dated 1/14/96
    f. interviews with seven hotel employees
    g. photocopies no. 1-21 and
    h. comprehensive RPD Report 416293-17
    Correct?

A. Yes.

Q. How did you obtain these "relevant portions" of the record?

A. Counsel sent them to me.

Q. So, Counsel and not you made the decisions as to what was relevant?

A. Yes.

Q. Do you know how many hundreds of pages of the depositions were not sent to you?

A. No.

Q. Could anything contained in these missing deposition pages or other records have had an impact on your factual assumptions or your ultimate opinion?

A. I don't know.

Q. That is because you never saw them, correct?

A. Yes.

Q. Might your opinion be different if you had an opportunity to review these missing records?

A. It might be.

Q. Did you request these missing records?

A. Yes.

Q. Why were they not provided to you?

A. I don't know.

Lesson: This is a very effective cross-examination in which the factual basis of the expert's opinion has been called into question. Experts who insist on and obtain complete copies of relevant documents are in a much stronger position to support their factual assumptions and ultimate opinions. When records and other documents are excerpted and "relevant" or "pertinent" portions are selected out by counsel or others, the expert may be deprived of crucial information, data, or facts. In addition, counsel has in effect substituted his judgment for that of the expert. The jury or fact finder is left to draw the conclusion that the lawyer may be intentionally omitting information that does not support the opinion he is seeking from the expert.

Example 6.510: Karnack the Magnificent

Q. As I understand it, you were sent a 240-page deposition transcript to review by Attorney Baker and you reviewed about 40 pages of the "relevant" material, correct?

A. Yes.

Q. You of course read the other 200 pages to see if it was relevant?

A. No.

Q. Could you explain how you determined that the 200 pages you didn't read were not relevant?

A. Well, experience – I have been in this business for 32 years.

Q. Let me see then, did you (counsel takes transcript and puts it against his forehead) hold the transcript pages like Karnack the Magnificent and say, "not relevant, not relevant, relevant"? Is that what your experience allows you to do?

Lesson: Experts cannot know whether a portion of a document is *relevant* unless they read that portion of the document. Counsel's cross-examination here may have been a little over the top, but the point is valid and is likely to be understood by the jury: How can the expert know if something is relevant if he hasn't read it? If the expert didn't even read everything that he was sent, why should a jury trust his opinion?

Numbers, figures, and formulas

Jurors and many people in general may have a hard time understanding or may be suspicious of statistics, numbers, figures, formulas, and other "math." It is crucial that experts not increase this suspicion. Experts who testify regarding numbers, figures, and formulas need to know their origins and understand specifically how they were derived. Counsel can be expected to attack any lack of familiarity or knowledge with numbers, figures, or formulas head-on during cross-examination. If the expert does not know the numbers cold, the jurors may ask the question, "Why should we trust that expert's numbers? It doesn't look like he even understands them." Please consider the following example:

Example 6.511: Fuzzy math

Q. In tab 5 or section 5 of your testimony, Mr. Neidermyer, you explain to us the, how we get to this 12 percent return on surplus standard. And just to summarize, I understand that it initially starts with a 10.4 arithmetic average of P & C Carriers over a 10-year period which is then rounded down to 10.2 [sic] and multiplied by 1.2?

A. I believe so, that is my understanding.

Q. When you say it is your understanding, are you saying you are not totally comfortable with it?

A. From the Nationwide, that is the way I understand that it was derived.

Q. Have you ever talked to—who came up with that number, do you know?

A. I am not sure.

Q. And your knowledge of how it was derived is in reading the Nationwide adjudication?

A. Yes. And well, in conversation with, several people in the Department.

Q. But you never talked to the person, whoever it was who actually came up with this number?

A. No.

...

Q. Now, if we, 10.4, well, the conversion formula is to take the GAAP equity figure, times it by 1.2 to give us a return on statutory surplus?

A. Correct.

Q. 10.4 can be multiplied by 1.2 can it not?

A. Correct.

Q. And that would give us 12.48? Is that right?

A. OK.

Q. Have you given any thought to why 12.48 … wasn't used as the Department's benchmark given that that would be the accurate transaction of this 10.4 percent figure that was derived from this ISO study apparently?

A. Early on when I was involved with this, it goes back very close to the beginning, I recall the 10.4 was based on actual data from the first report and then the 1988 results actually slipped a bit. And I believe it was my thought that that was the reason the 10 percent was selected and then the 1.2 applied to that.

Q. But I take it your testimony is that you are not real clear that that is what happened?

A. No.

Q. You have this vague recollection?

A. Right.

Q. So other than this vague recollection there is no reason that you know of why the number that the Department calculated to be the average return earned by the property/casualty insurance industry from 1979 through 1988, shouldn't be the 10.4 figure which apparently it was?

A. No.

Q. It simply was rounded down to 10.0?

A. Correct.

Q. If you were going to indicate what would be an adequate rate of return on a going basis for a company, P&C writer [sic] today, would you recommend in your professional judgment a 12 percent on statutory surplus?

A. I have not done any studies so that I would feel comfortable with picking a number.

Q. Do you recall testifying in the Liberty Mutual case that you would not be sure if you would accept 12 percent on a going basis as being a fair and adequate rate?

A. I recall.

Q. Has anything changed your mind from your testimony in that hearing to today's hearing?

A. No.

Lesson: In the above example, the court rejected the 12% threshold based in large part on the ambiguity and uncertainty of the expert's testimony. Experts should be prepared to explain in detail and with precision how they arrive at rates, numbers, figures, and formulas. Failure to do so will, as in the above example, have disastrous results.

For additional information on the above example, see *Prudential Property and Casualty Insurance Company v. Department of Insurance*, 595 A.2d 649 (Pa. Cmwlth 1991).

Passage of time between accident and inspection

Experts who conduct an inspection of a machine, accident scene, or anything else long after the accident date can expect to be cross-examined concerning the passage of time and its effect on the item at issue. This is a legitimate area of inquiry. At issue, of course, is whether the conditions were substantially the same at the time of the inspection as they were at the time of the incident. If there is a reason why the expert does not believe that conditions have changed substantially, the expert should be prepared to explain this. Please consider the following example:

Example 6.512: Golf car inspection made 4 years after accident

Q. You inspected the golf car in question how many years after the accident?

A. Approximately four years.

Q. You found that the set screw that connects the directional lever to the control shaft was improperly positioned?

A. Yes.

Q. Has the set screw of the golf car in question been modified in any way since the accident?

A. Not to my knowledge.

Q. Was the key switch tightened during the intervening four years?

A. Not to my knowledge.

Q. The golf car was put back into use after the accident, was it not?

A. Yes.

Q. What repairs were made to it before it was put back into use?

A. I don't know.

Q. How many different people drove the car in the intervening four years?

A. I am not sure.

Q. What maintenance was done to the golf car over the four years?

A. I don't know. There was no service record available.

Q. So you cannot say with a reasonable degree of engineering certainty that the set screw was not changed and the golf car remained in substantially the same condition four years after the accident when you examined it?

Lesson: This is an effective cross-examination. It calls into question the expert's entire opinion. If the expert in this example had reason to believe that the set screw had not been altered, it would have been beneficial to explain this during direct, or, if given an opportunity, during cross-examination.

This example was based on the case of *Tidemann v. Nadler Golf Car Sales, Inc.*, 224 F.3rd 719 (7 Cir. 2000).

Amount of time spent on case

Experts should anticipate being questioned on the amount of time they have spent on the case. Counsel can attempt to imply or prove that the expert did any of the following.

- He spent too many hours in an attempt to run up a large bill. The expert is therefore dishonest and will defraud or lie for money. He could not have spent all of the hours he alleges. The expert is therefore dishonest, sloppy, or forgetful. In any event, he is not to be believed.

- He is mistaken about the time spent due to discrepancies between his testimony and his billing records. If the expert doesn't even know how many hours he spent on the matter or can't get his billing straight, why should he be believed when giving an opinion?

- He spent too little time before reaching his opinions. Was there a rush to judgment? Was there an adequate investigation?

If counsel is successful in any of these endeavors, the expert and his opinion will be less believable. To blunt such inquiries, experts should do the following.

- Conduct a thorough investigation, but not pad their bills.

- Be prepared to answer questions about the amount of time spent on the matter, including the hours billed to date. This number should conform to the expert's billing records.

- Be prepared to justify and explain why the expert spent a relatively small or large amount of time on the case.

Please consider the following examples:

Example 6.513: Opinion in products liability case formed after only 4 hours of records review

Q. Doctor, as I understand it, you are offering three opinions in this electrocution case:

   1.   that the design of the Wayne Model CDU 800 sump pump is defective in that the strain relief mechanism is inadequate to secure the power cord in the watertight seal during foreseeable uses of the pump;

2.   that the breach of the watertight seal caused the decedent's elec-
      trocution, and

3.   that the decedent experienced severe pain as well as other effects
      of electrical shock.

Correct?

A. Yes.

Q. You reached your conclusions after spending only four hours review-
    ing documents in your office?

A. Yes. I did everything necessary to formulate my opinions in this case.

Lesson: This was a very effective cross-examination. The jury is likely to
be suspicious of an expert opinion where the expert merely quickly
reviewed some documents and never even made a physical inspection of
the item in question. A more thorough investigation or at least a better
explanation of why a longer investigation was not done would have
helped this expert. For example, in response to counsel's last question, the
expert might have responded, if appropriate, "Yes. This case is basically
identical to an electrocution case involving a CDU 800 I handled just last
year. As a result, it was not necessary to duplicate most of my research and
I was able to reach a conclusion much more quickly than usual."

The above example is based on the case of *Traharne v. Wayne/Sott Fetzer
Company*, 156 F.Supp.2d 697 (N.D. Ill. 2001). In that case, the court
expressed its concern with the limited time spent by the expert:

> At the outside, it must be noted that Dr. Morse reached
> his conclusions "after spending only four hours review-
> ing documents in his office in San Diego." Dr. Morse was
> of the opinion that he had done everything necessary to
> formulate his opinions in this case. The amount of time
> and work expended by an expert in familiarizing himself
> with a particular case; in culling key facts from the doc-
> umentation presented to him; and in developing the fac-
> tual predicate for his opinions clearly goes to his appro-
> priate case, the amount of time and work expended may
> also go to the issue of whether or not the expert's opin-
> ion is predicated on a reliable methodology or tech-

nique. Although the limited time expended by Dr. Morse is troubling, given his expertise and background, it may well be sufficient. In any event, we believe that sound discretion dictates that we permit the trier of fact to take into account the time expended by him when weighing and considering his opinion testimony. At 707-708.

Example 6.514: More time reading a deposition than the actual deposition took

Q. You were asked by counsel to determine if Mr. Fitz stopped at the red light or drove thorough it immediately prior to the accident, correct?

A. Yes. That was what I was asked to determine.

Q. You charge by the hour, correct?

A. Yes.

Q. How much per hour?

A. $200 an hour for my accident reconstruction work.

Q. Your bill came to a total of $20,000 in this case.

A. Yes.

Q. You spent, according to your invoice, 28 hours reading depositions?

A. Yes.

Q. Are you aware that was seven times the time the actual depositions themselves took?

A. No, I am not.

Q. Is it your testimony that it took you 28 hours to read four depositions totaling 120 pages?

A. Well, I read, re-read and analyzed them.

Q. You spent seven hours reviewing the 28 photographs?

A. If that's what the invoice says.

Q. Can you please hand me your contemporaneous time sheets in this case?

A. I don't have any.

Q. Is it fair to say that your $20,000 bill is an estimate of what you felt your testimony was worth to the plaintiff in this case?

Lesson: One thing jurors certainly understand and can relate to is overcharging or selling out for money. Although jurors expect experts to be well paid, an outlandish bill, as in the above example, will open the expert up to effective cross-examination.

Example 6.515: 27 hours billed in a day

Q. Sir, we have subpoenaed your billing records for the period of 1999-2001 and you produced these records, correct?

A. Yes – and I might add it was costly and time consuming to comply with the subpoena.

Q. As a sole practitioner, sir, can you explain to the jury how you billed a total of 412 hours on four cases on 9/19/99?

A. I was working like a dog, Counsel.

Q. When you billed 27 hours on one day, 32 on another day, and 48 hours on a third day in October of 2001, I guess you were working like two dogs?

Lesson: Experts who overbill will suffer credibility problems. Obviously, in an extreme case like this, something is wrong. Either the expert is a fraud, a lunatic, or very, very sloppy in his bookkeeping. Note how the attorney in this case researched the expert's billings in other cases in an effort to dig up dirt on the expert.

Example 6.516: Discrepancies between billing records and time sheets

Q. You testified that on 7/14/2001 you went to the accident scene for approximately 4 hours?

A. Correct.

Q. Are you aware that your billing records indicate you spent eight hours at the scene?

A. Well, it could have included travel.

Q. That was four hours to go 12 miles. The traffic was pretty bad that day?

A. I don't recall.

Q. Are you aware of the fact that there are 27 unexplained discrepancies between your testimony and your billing records?

A. No, but I am sure I can explain.

Q. Excellent, let's put the first one on the overhead projector. Can you explain the difference here, sir?

Lesson: The jury is being asked to draw the conclusion that either this expert is sloppy or dishonest. An expert should review his billing records as part of the preparation process to make sure his testimony is consistent with the records. If his testimony is inconsistent, he should be prepared to explain why there is a discrepancy.

Reliance on other experts

Experts are generally permitted to base their opinions in part or in whole on reliable facts or data that are not themselves in evidence. These facts and data relied upon generally need not themselves even be admissible in evidence. Federal Rule of Evidence 703 provides:

Rule 703. Bases of Opinion Testimony by Experts

> The facts or data in the particular case upon which an expert bases an opinion or inference may be those perceived by or made known to the expert at or before the hearing. If of a type reasonably relied upon by experts in the particular field in forming opinions or inferences upon the subject, the facts or data need not be admissible in evidence in order for the opinion or inference to be admitted. Facts or data that are otherwise inadmissible shall not be disclosed to the jury by the proponent

of the opinion or inference unless the court determines that their probative value in assisting the jury to evaluate the expert's opinion substantially outweighs their prejudicial effect.

Because an expert's opinion is only as strong as the facts and data upon which it is based, experts can expect to be closely cross-examined on all the facts and data upon which they based their opinion. This includes the opinions of other experts that the testifying expert relied upon. Counsel will try to prove two things:

- that the expert's opinion depends upon the opinion of another expert, and
- that the expert has no way of knowing the accuracy of the other expert's opinion.

Please consider the following example:

Example 6.517: Physician relies on radiologist

Q. Doctor, as I understand it, you found that the MRI of Ms. Haramd was negative, correct?

A. Yes, that's correct.

Q. Doctor, isn't it true that you didn't actually review the film of the MRI, but relied on the finding of the radiologist, Dr. Ryan?

A. That's true.

Q. Isn't it good medical practice before rendering an opinion to review the actual films so you can reach your own conclusions, Doctor?

A. Well, yes, but sometimes due to time pressure we rely on the radiologist's report.

Q. Doctor, did you even try to obtain and review the films?

A. No.

Q. Would a review of the films themselves change your opinion, Doctor?

A. I don't know. I haven't seen them, so I can't say.

Q. As you are not a radiologist, you would defer to an expert in reading these films, would you not?

A. Well, I would prefer to read them myself.

Q. But you didn't read the films yourself, correct, Doctor?

A. Correct.

Q. And you don't know if the radiologist made a mistake in reading the film, do you?

Lesson: Experts often rely on the reports and expertise of other experts. There is nothing wrong with this. The most damning admission in this case was that the expert didn't ask to see the films himself. That makes him look like he rushed into judgment. In many cases, it is perfectly reasonable to rely on other experts. The reasons for this should be brought to the attention of the jury. For example, "Dr. Ryan is the chief of Radiology at University Hospital. He is very well respected in his field and I have worked with him on numerous occasions. I trust his work and I have no reason to suspect his reading of the films was in error. It was my impression that the films were not available. Had I thought they were available, I would have reviewed them personally."

Degree of certainty: terms such as "possible" and "conceivable"

Experts should expect to be cross-examined about the degree of certainty they possess while expressing their opinion. How sure is the expert? Does the expert merely have a hunch? Generally, a reasonable degree of certainty is what is required. Experts should express their opinions "to a reasonable degree of (medical, engineering, appraisal, etc.) certainty." When an expert uses other words to express or describe her degree of certainty, she may run into trouble. Please consider the following examples.

Example 6.518: "In my opinion she had it, but possibly"

Q. Dr. Harris, within a reasonable degree of medical certainty, did Ms. Montgomery have or did she not have Crohn's Disease in January of '87?

A. I can't answer that absolutely.

Q. We are not asking for an absolute answer. We are saying within a reasonable degree of medical certainty.

A. I still can't answer it except possibly or probably. In my opinion she
had it, but possibly.

Lesson: The above testimony actually took place on direct examination in
the case of *Montgomery v. Butler*, 834 S.W.2d. 148 (Ark. 1992). Retaining
counsel first asked his expert:

> Whether Mrs. Montgomery had Crohn's disease in
> January 1987, to which Dr. Harris replied that "[s]he
> probably did." Dr. Butler's counsel objected on the
> ground that the question and the answer were not stat-
> ed "to a reasonable degree of certainty or probability."

> Retaining counsel then rephrased the question and
> obtained the "she had it, but possibly" answer. The
> answer "she had it, but possibly" was left to stand by the
> court because opposing counsel failed to object in a
> timely fashion. *All of this difficulty could have been
> avoided if the expert had been properly prepared to
> state his opinion "to a reasonable degree of medical
> certainty."*

Example 6.519: "Conceivable"

Q. Now, in degrees of certainty, do you have varying degrees?

A. Yes.

Q. What is conceivable?

A. It's on the positive side, but not too high.

Q. And what is after conceivable?

A. Probable, highly probable and identified going up the ladder.

Q. That's the bottom of the spectrum, conceivable.

A. And common authorship would be less than that.

Q. So, you cannot say to a degree of scientific certainty in your field of
endeavor that this, in fact, was the handwriting of Mr. Bertram?

A. Not based on what I had at that time. That was the signature, not the handprinting.

Lesson: Experts should be fully conversant with the legally sufficient and acceptable degrees of certainty and the methods of expressing them in their particular field. This example (in which the questioning cited above was done by the trial judge) was based upon the case of *State v. Bertram*, 591 A.2d 14 (R.I. 1991). The court found the expert's testimony that it was "conceivable" that the signature on the hotel registration form could have been written by the defendant was admissible because defense counsel had ample opportunity to cross-examine the witness on his conclusions and emphasize any infirmities pertaining to his analysis of the signature.

Standard of care

In medical malpractice cases, the medical standard of care expert can expect to be asked how he defines "standard of care" and how he arrived at his opinion as to what the standard of care was. In terms of defining the standard of care, experts should work with retaining counsel so that the expert knows the standard that applies in the case at hand. The expert needs to be aware that this opinion may not be admissible and will certainly be challenged on cross-examination if it is based on the expert's personal opinion, speculation, or conjecture. Opinions regarding standard of care, as well as all other opinions, should be backed up by research and facts to be persuasive. This needs to be done before the expert takes the stand. Once on the stand, experts need to be prepared to justify the reasons for their opinions. Please consider the following example:

Example 6.520: Where was standard of care defined?

During cross-examination, in response to questions about fetal heart rate and fetal growth, Dr. Hill generally mentioned literature, meetings, national meetings, and the American College as bases for his opinion. He was asked about the frequency with which physicians documented growth. He asserted, in response, that "a two-week interval is the standard that I use and many other physicians do, as well." He was then asked the following questions.

Q. Well doctor,…you're saying that's the national standard, doctor?

A. It's the standard I've always heard of.

Q. You just heard that around the D.C. area? You've heard that through your colleagues in the local area, right, doctor?

A. Literature, meetings.

Q. In the local area?

A. No. National meetings, American College.

After indicating that he was familiar with the work of Dr. Steven G. Gabbe, Obstetrics, Normal and Problem Pregnancies, Dr. Hill was asked:

Q. You would agree … that Dr. Gabbe has identified five sonographic criteria for the almost unequivocal diagnosis of twin-to-twin transfusion syndrome?

A. I've not read that particular passage.

Lesson: This example was based upon the case of *Hawes v. Chua*, 769 A.2d 797 (Dist. of Col. 2001). In that case, opposing counsel objected to the national standard of care testimony as being legally insufficient and inadmissible. The appeals court barely upheld the admission of the testimony, stating:

> We conclude that the trial judge's decision not to strike his testimony did not constitute manifest error. However, we stress that while the trial judge retains considerable discretion in determining whether to admit defense national standard of care expert testimony,
>
> 1. It is insufficient for the expert to merely recite the words "national standard of care;"
>
> 2. The expert's testimony may not be based on his or her personal opinion, nor on mere speculation or conjecture; and
>
> 3. The expert's opinion must reflect some evidence of a national standard, such as attendance at national seminars or meetings or conventions, or reference to published materials, when assessing a medical course of action or treatment. At 805.

During their preparation with retaining counsel, experts should carefully review the applicable standard of care. An expert opinion should be based on reliable methodology and experts should be prepared to precisely and articulately recite the methodology used (for example, "At the American College's 1995 meeting this very issue was presented by...Furthermore, the Practice Guidelines published by the College clearly state that..."). This was not done in this case and the expert's entire opinion was almost thrown out.

CHAPTER 11

Forensic Accountants and Attorney-Client Privilege

Carl Pacini, William Hillison and Steven Thompson

Under certain conditions, a lawyer may shield a non-testifying forensic accountant under the *Kovel* rule. This rule extends the attorney-client privilege to forensic accountant-client communications and work product when the forensic accountant is hired to help in the rendition of legal services. The party claiming the privilege bears the burden of proving the existence of the various factors required to sustain it. Various protective measures reviewed in this article are vital to preserve the extension of the privilege to forensic accountants. Attorneys and forensic accountants should also be concerned about the risks of inadvertent disclosure and eavesdropping from the use of e-mail, cellular phones, and faxes. In some cases, inadvertent disclosure leads to the loss of the attorney-client privilege. We suggest numerous steps to minimize the likelihood of loss of the privilege.

Imagine a forensic accountant[1] who has been engaged by an attorney as a non- testifying consultant[2] regarding an alleged false billing scheme per-

---

[1] We use the term "forensic accountant" to represent accountants and fraud examiners acting as experts or consultants to third parties in litigation, administrative proceedings, or investigations.

[2] Communications and work product involving an expert who testifies are generally accessible or "discoverable" by an adversary in a judicial proceeding. An expert witness should be insulated from the client as much as possible and limited to "need to know" information about the case (Spiro and Rule 1994).

Carl Pacini is Associate Professor of Accounting and Business Law, Florida Gulf Coast University, Ft. Myers, FL. William Hillison is Andersen Professor of Accounting, Florida State University, Tallahassee, FL. Steven Thompson is Professor of Accounting, Texas State University, San Marcos, TX.

petrated by an employee of one of the attorney's clients. Barring various criminal violations, the forensic accountant's workpapers and communications with the attorney should be protected from disclosure by the attorney-client privilege. The latter relates to the protection of confidential communications between an attorney and a client in a trial or administrative/judicial proceeding.

In some jurisdictions, the privilege may be waived because of inadvertent disclosure of privileged information during the use of electronic communications (e.g., cellular phones, e-mail). Such a waiver may result in malpractice liability for the expert and undesirable costs and consequences for the client. Therefore, it is vital for forensic accountants to be familiar with the attorney-client privilege and its limitations to better serve clients and minimize potential legal liability. The purposes of this article are to examine the application and extension of the attorney-client privilege to forensic accountants who serve as non-testifying experts and/or consultants and to suggest practical ways to help protect the privilege from challenge.[3]

The next two sections outline the shortcomings of the accountant-client privilege and provide an overview of the attorney-client privilege. The fourth section describes the conditions under which the doctrine is extended to forensic accountants and other consultants/experts involved in litigation cases, and provides practical guidance, based on previous case law, regarding the measures that forensic accountants (hired by attorneys to assist in a legal matter) must take to increase the likelihood of securing the protection of the attorney-client privilege. The fifth section discusses the risks posed to the attorney-client privilege by the use of electronic communications. The final section provides concluding comments.

SHORTCOMINGS OF THE ACCOUNTANT-CLIENT PRIVILEGE

From a forensic accountant's perspective, the inability to protect or insulate communications and work product from disclosure threatens client openness and the ability to deliver quality services (Segal 1997). Despite the

---

[3] We do not offer legal advice. Parties affected by issues related to privileged communications should seek competent legal counsel.

existence of accountant-client privilege statutes in some states, such statutes are of dubious value to the forensic accountant-client relationship (Causey and Causey 1999). The accountant-client privilege is not recognized under federal common law and does not attach to communications between the client and accountant. Moreover, state accountant-client privilege statutes may not be applied in federal cases (Corcoran 2000; Molony 1998).[4]

Despite the difficulties associated with the accountant-client privilege, forensic accountant-client communications and work product[5] may still be insulated from disclosure when a forensic accountant works as an agent of an attorney rendering legal services. Under certain conditions, such communications and work product are protected by the attorney-client privilege.

OVERVIEW OF THE ATTORNEY-CLIENT PRIVILEGE

Federal Rule of Evidence 501 is the basis for the attorney-client privilege in federal courts. The rule provides that "the privilege of a witness ... shall be governed by the principles of the common law as they may be interpreted by the courts of the United States in light of reason and experience." The attorney-client privilege is the oldest privilege established by common law. In the early 1600s, the attorney-client privilege evolved as an extension of the individual's right to avoid self-incrimination. The privilege developed to preclude an attorney from having to testify against his client. Originally, the privilege attached or belonged to the attorney but today is considered to belong to the client.[6] However, the attorney can raise the privilege on the client's behalf.[7]

---

[4] In *Couch v. U.S.*, 409 U.S. 322 (1973), Justice Powell allowed the IRS to enforce a summons and mandated that the accountant turn over business records used in preparing tax returns. The Supreme Court denied protection because the expectation of confidentiality in an accountant-client relationship was an insufficient justification as the records were pertinent to the tax returns (Corcoran 2000).

[5] The work product privilege is contained in the Federal Rules of Civil Procedure and provides that documents prepared in anticipation of litigation or trial are not subject to discovery without a showing of substantial need and undue hardship. Fed. R. Civ. P. 26 (b) (3). In *U.S. v. Arthur Young*, 465 U.S. 805 (1984), the Supreme Court ruled that accountants had no work product privilege.

[6] *U.S. v. Bilzerian*, 926 F.2d 1285 (2d Cir. 1991).

[7] *In the Matter of a Grand Jury Subpoena Duces Tecum*, 391 F.Supp. 1029 (S.D.N.Y. 1975).

Proposed Rule of Evidence 503, also known as Supreme Court Standard 503, sets the general parameters for determining the scope of the privilege under federal common law:

A client has a privilege to refuse to disclose and to prevent any other person from disclosing confidential communications made for the purpose of facilitating the rendition of professional legal services to the client. The communications can be

- between the client or client's representative and his attorney or the attorney's representative;

- between the client's lawyer and that lawyer's representative;

- by the client or his lawyer to a lawyer representing another in a matter of common interest;

- between representatives of the client; or

- between lawyers representing the client.

The privilege must be claimed with regard to a particular communication and extends only to a communication and not to facts.[8] A client may not refuse to disclose a relevant fact within his knowledge merely because he incorporated a statement of such fact into a communication with his attorney.[9] An attorney's communication to a client reporting facts learned by the attorney from a third party is not within the attorney-client privilege unless the information is included in legal analysis or advice communicated to the client.[10] The privilege may be waived unless it is claimed before any disclosure of the communication sought to be protected (Jones 1998). If a client communicates a matter to his lawyer in the presence of a third

---

[8] *U.S. v. United Shoe Mach. Corp.*, 89 F.Supp. 357 (D. Mass. 1950); *Shiner v. American Stock Exch.*, 28 F.R.D. 34 (S.D.N.Y. 1961).

[9] *Upjohn v. U.S.*, 449 U.S. 383 (1981).

[10] The critical inquiry is whether, viewing the lawyer's communication in its full content and context, it was made in order to render legal advice or services to the client. *ECDC Environmental, L.C. v. New York Marine and General Ins. Co.*, 1998 U.S. Dist. Lexis 8808 (S.D.N.Y. 1998).

party who is not an agent of the lawyer, the communication is not confidential. The assumption is that the nature of the communication demonstrates that the client did not intend for the communication to be kept confidential.[11] One exception to the privilege waiver is the joint defense or common interest rule which protects the confidentiality of communications between multiple parties and their attorneys when such parties share a common legal interest.[12]

Various tests have been set forth by courts to determine whether the attorney-client privilege applies to a particular case. Each test, however, requires that the party claiming the privilege prove the existence of each of the following elements:

1. The holder of the privilege is or sought to become a client;

2. The person to whom a communication is made is a licensed attorney or his agent;

3. The attorney is acting as the client's lawyer with regard to the communication; and

4. The communication relates to a matter of which the attorney was informed by his client, without the presence of third parties, for the purpose of securing legal services and not for the purpose of committing a crime or a tort.[13]

Although each element above must be supported by facts, deciding whether the attorney-client privilege exists is done on a case-by-case basis by the application of common sense.

---

[11] In *re John Doe Corporation*, 675 F.2d 482 (2d Cir. 1982); *U.S. v. Gurtner*, 474 F.2d 297 (9th Cir. 1973); *In re Von Bulow*, 828 F.2d 94 (2d Cir. 1987).

[12] It is unnecessary that there be actual litigation in progress for the joint defense or common interest rule of the attorney-client privilege to apply. *U.S. v. Zolin*, 809 F.2d 1411 (9th Cir. 1987), vacated in part on other grounds, 842 F.2d 1135 (9th Cir. 1988)(en banc), aff'd in part and vacated in part on other grounds, 491 U.S. 554 (1989); *Walsh v. Northrop Grumman Corp.*, 165 F.R.D. 16 (E.D.N.Y. 1996).

[13] *U.S. v. United Shoe Mach. Corp.*, 89 F.Supp. 357 (D. Mass. 1950); *Colton v. U.S.*, 306 F.2d 633 (2d Cir. 1962), *cert.den.* 371 U.S. 951 (1963).

The attorney-client privilege may also be asserted by a corporation or other business organization, not just an individual. Application of the privilege to corporations, including situations involving in-house counsel, has been problematic because corporations can act only through their agents. In *Upjohn v. U.S.*,[14] the Supreme Court faced the question of which corporate employees could claim attorney-client privilege on behalf of the corporation. In response to a government criminal investigation involving bribery allegations, Upjohn declined to produce various documents demanded by the IRS. The court held that the documents were protected by the attorney-client privilege. Interestingly, the court rejected the IRS' argument that in order for the privilege to apply, an employee must be a member of the "control group" of a client – those with decision-making authority. Although the court did not draft a set of formal criteria for all situations involving the attorney-client privilege in the corporate setting, the following set of guidelines was offered for application on a case-by-case basis:

> A communication is privileged when an employee or former employee speaks at the direction of management with an attorney regarding conduct or proposed conduct within the scope of employment. The attorney must be one authorized by management to inquire into the subject and must be seeking information to assist counsel in ... (a) evaluating whether the employee's conduct has bound or would bind the corporation; (b) assessing the legal consequences, if any, of that conduct; and (c) formulating appropriate legal responses to actions that have been taken or may be taken...[15]

The protection afforded by the attorney-client privilege is limited to those situations where the communication would not have been made but for the client's need for legal advice or services (Sexton 1982). The *Upjohn* decision left no doubt that the privilege also applies to in-house counsel, but lower courts have disagreed on the scope of the privilege (Hill 1995).

---

[14] 449 U.S. 383 (1981).
[15] 449 U.S. at 403.

In-house counsel often has dual business and legal responsibilities within a corporation. Under *Hardy*,[16] when a corporate decision is based on both a business policy and a legal evaluation, the business aspects of that decision are not protected by the privilege simply because legal considerations are involved. Moreover, it has been argued that in-house counsel was being held to a higher standard than outside counsel for attorney-client privilege to attach. Outside counsel does not face a higher standard because an outside attorney lacks business responsibilities within a corporation. Without a higher standard, any business advice would fall within attorney-client privilege (Jones 1998).

ATTORNEY-CLIENT PRIVILEGE EXTENDED TO FORENSIC ACCOUNTANTS AND OTHERS

The first subsection below reviews the landmark *Kovel* case, which extended attorney-client privilege to third parties hired by a lawyer or client to assist in providing legal services to the client. The second subsection examines the *Adlman* case in which the court refused to extend the *Kovel* privilege due to inadequate documentation to support the privilege. The third subsection outlines a number of steps, based on case law, that forensic auditors should implement to ensure privilege is intact in their work as non-testifying consultants hired by attorneys to assist in legal matters. Table 1 includes a list of important safeguards that should be followed to protect the *Kovel* privilege.

The *Kovel* Privilege

A lawyer may cloak a non-testifying expert or consultant with the protection of the attorney-client privilege. The landmark decision in *U.S. v. Kovel*[17] extended the attorney-client privilege to communications between a client and an accountant hired by an attorney to assist in providing legal services. Louis Kovel was a former IRS agent with accounting skills hired by a law firm to assist in advising the firm's clients. Kovel met with a client who was under IRS investigation for tax fraud and received the client's personal financial statement along with a cover letter indicat-

---

[16] *Hardy v. New York News, Inc.*, 114 F.R.D. 633 (S.D.N.Y. 1987).
[17] 296 F.2d 918 (2d Cir. 1961).

Table 1.
Recommended Safeguards to Preserve the Kovel Privilege

Safeguard	Description/Reason
Client retains attorney who then hires forensic accountant (or client first consults with both the lawyer and forensic accountant simultaneously).	The Kovel privilege does not apply to those cases in which the client communicates first with his own accountant and then with his lawyer. This distinction prevents the privilege from being unduly expanded.
The privilege requires that the communication must be made for the purpose of assisting in giving legal advice to the client.	If the forensic accountant's advice is sought rather than legal advice then the Kovel privilege does not apply. Even legal advice is unprivileged if it is incidental to business advice.
The party claiming the Kovel privilege must prepare and retain adequate documentation to support the claim. The documentation must show that the main purpose in hiring the forensic accountant or other expert was to assist an attorney in providing legal advice.	The burden is on the party claiming the Kovel privilege to justify its application in a given case. The reason is that the common law favors disclosure and does not promote policies or privileges that hinder it.
The Kovel privilege even applies to independent contractors hired to assist an attorney in rendering legal services. Any privileged communication must be within the scope of the consultant's duties and may not be disseminated beyond those who need to know.	It is inappropriate to distinguish between third parties on the client's payroll and those hired as independent contractors.
The client's existing accountant should not be hired to perform forensic accounting services (unless absolutely necessary).	Use of the existing accountant makes it more difficult to establish that he was hired primarily to help the attorney render legal advice.
If the client's existing accountant is hired matters covered by the Kovel privilege should be segregated.	This step is necessary to dispel the argument that the Kovel engagement was part of an overall package of services.
In the case of a corporation, outside or in-house counsel, not management, should hire the forensic accountant.	A higher standard to invoke the attorney-client privilege is applied to in-house counsel.
The attorney-forensic accountant arrangement should be documented by a well-drafted engagement letter. The agreement should state that the forensic accountant is being hired in anticipation of litigation and that all communications are incidental to rendering legal services. Forensic accountants should bill or invoice the law firm directly.	An engagement letter minimizes the likelihood of a misunderstanding among the parties and serves as foundation for claiming Kovel rule protection. Direct billing creates a paper audit trail that shows compliance with recommended safeguards to preserve the attorney-client privilege.
The forensic accountant and client may communicate outside counsel's presence but may only do so at counsel's direction.	In U.S. v. Bein, a federal appeals court ruled that the Kovel rule did not apply to a conversation between an accountant and a client outside client's presence.
In the case of a corporation, a top management written directive should state that any communications between employees and a forensic accountant hired by are made pursuant to management's instructions and should not be disclosed to any third party.	Intentional or unintentional disclosure of any communication(s) or work product may result in a waiver of the Kovel privilege.
The attorney-forensic accountant engagement agreement should state that all documents, including working papers, are the property of the lawyer and are to be returned at the lawyer's request. Forensic accountant work product should be furnished to counsel not the client.	One federal appeals court held that attorney-client privilege may be waived involuntarily.
Forensic accountant "work product" should be labeled "protected by the attorney-client and work product privileges."	Use of such a label does not insure protection under attorney-client privilege but serves as notice.

ing the purpose for sending the statement. After being subpoenaed by a grand jury, Kovel refused to answer questions about his conversations with the client and the effect of the transactions. Kovel was held in contempt of court and sentenced to a year in prison.

The Second Circuit Court of Appeals reversed the contempt citation and ruled that the presence of an accountant as an attorney's agent does not negate the attorney-client privilege. The court noted that because of the "complexities of modern existence" few lawyers could operate without the aid of secretaries, clerks, telephone operators, law clerks and others. No reason could be found to exclude accountants from the list of those who assist lawyers in providing legal services. The court ruled that the privilege shields communications with an accountant retained by the lawyer or client to assist in providing legal services to the attorney's client.

The court decision attempts to define the boundaries of the *Kovel* privilege. The court acknowledged that an arbitrary line was being drawn between a case in which the client communicates first with his own accountant and then later consults with his lawyer (no privilege) and one in which the client initially retains an attorney who then hires an accountant or the client first consults with both the lawyer and accountant simultaneously (privilege exists). In *U.S. v. Cote*,[18] the court made clear that communications from client to accountant made prior to the accountant being hired by an attorney are not privileged. This distinction is necessary to prevent the privilege from being unduly expanded.

It is paramount to the privilege that the communication be made in confidence for the purpose of obtaining legal advice from the attorney. If the accountant's advice is what is sought rather than legal advice, no privilege attaches. Even legal advice is unprivileged if it is merely incidental to business advice.[19] One federal appeals court applied the *Kovel* rule to memoranda and a financial statement prepared by an accountant hired by an attorney because the former's role was to "facilitate an accurate and complete consultation between the client and attorney about the client's financial condition."[20]

---

[18] 456 F.2d 142 (8th Cir. 1972).

[19] *Durham Industries, Inc. v. North River Ins. Co.*, 1980 U.S. Dist. Lexis 15154 (S.D.N.Y. 1980).

[20] *U.S. v. Judson*, 322 F.2d 460 (9th Cir. 1963).

Document the Privilege

In *U.S. v. Adlman*,[21] Sequa Corporation's in-house counsel (Adlman) hired Arthur Andersen (AA), the firm's auditor, to prepare a memorandum of the tax consequences of a proposed corporate reorganization. The draft and final AA memoranda were delivered to in-house counsel after discussions between AA and Adlman. Two days after delivery of the final memorandum to in-house counsel, AA sent a summary and recommendations directly to Sequa's management. Sequa consummated the transaction as recommended by AA. Sequa, claiming attorney-client privilege, refused to produce the AA memorandum in response to an IRS subpoena.

Sequa argued that it relied on in-house counsel for legal advice about the transaction and that the AA memorandum was prepared to aid in-house counsel in rendering legal advice. The Second Circuit Court of Appeals held that attorney-client privilege did not apply because the evidence indicated Sequa consulted an accounting firm for tax advice rather than in-house counsel receiving accounting advice to assist him in rendering legal advice. The court noted that Sequa had not produced adequate documentation, such as a separate retainer agreement or itemized billings, for the AA tax advice, to support a claim of privilege. The only evidence offered to uphold privilege was a series of affidavits prepared by interested parties four years after the transaction at issue. Thus, it is incumbent upon those claiming attorney-client privilege to prepare and produce adequate documentation to show that the main purpose in hiring the expert was to assist an attorney in providing legal services to support any claim of privilege.

The ruling in *Adlman* has implications for experts besides accountants as the *Kovel* rule has been extended to other third-party experts. Although few court decisions address *Kovel's* application to consultants other than accountants, it has been applied to communications with a psychiatrist assisting a lawyer in preparing a defense,[22] a bail bondsman,[23] an operator of a polygraph,[24] and a patent agent assisting an attorney[25] (Spiro and

---

[21] 68 F.3d 1495 (2d Cir. 1995).

[22] *U.S. v. Alvarez*, 519 F.2d 1036 (3d Cir. 1975).

[23] *In re Witness-Attorney before Grand Jury No. 83-1*, 613 F.Supp. 394 (S.D. Fla. 1984)

[24] *People v. George*, 428 N.Y.S.2d 825 (Sup. Ct. 1980).

[25] *Golden Trade S.r.L. v. Lee Apparel Co.*, 143 F.R.D. 514 (S.D.N.Y. 1992).

Rule 1994). Another court suggested that the privilege could apply in a situation where a research institute was hired by an attorney for TRW, Inc., a credit reporting agency, to prepare a study of the latter's computerized credit reporting system.[26]

Other Safeguards to Protect the Kovel Privilege

In a more recent case, *In re: Bieter Co.*,[27] a federal appeals court approved application of the attorney-client privilege to various communications between a law firm and a real estate consultant engaged by the client, a real estate developer. The real estate consultant was hired as an independent contractor under a written agreement during the initial phase of land development. The consultant worked with architects, engineers and counsel and appeared at meetings involving local government officials. The legal issue of attorney-client privilege was complicated by the consultant not being an employee of the client (a partnership).

In upholding the attorney-client privilege, the appeals court identified several factors in concluding that it is inappropriate to distinguish between those on the client's payroll and those employed as independent contractors. First, the communications in question were made for the purpose of seeking legal advice. Second, the third-party expert involved in communications did so at the direction of the client. Third, the subject matter of the communication was within the scope of the consultant's duties. Last, the communications were not disseminated beyond those parties who needed to know.

The *Bieter* decision is significant for third-party experts such as forensic accountants. However, the boundaries of the *Kovel* rule are tightly drawn and application of the privilege is strictly interpreted. A carelessly structured *Kovel* relationship can leave the attorney-client privilege vulnerable to attack (Spiro and Rule 1994; Riback 1999). Various common sense safeguards are essential in preserving the extension of the privilege to forensic accountants.

---

[26] *Federal Trade Commission v. TRW, Inc.*, 628 F.2d 207 (D.C. Cir. 1980).
[27] 16 F.3d 929 (8th Cir. 1994).

First, the attorney, and not the client, should hire the forensic accountant. Preferably, the client's existing accountant should not be hired to perform forensic accounting services (unless absolutely necessary). Use of the client's current accountant makes it more difficult to establish that he served as a litigation or legal assistant rather than as a financial advisor with regard to a particular communication. This problem is compounded if the accountant is called to testify (Spiro and Rule 1994).

In the event counsel hires the client's present accountant, matters covered by the *Kovel* privilege should be adequately segregated to make plausible the argument that the *Kovel* engagement was not part of an overall package of services (Raby and Raby 1995). What this "chinese wall" actually requires depends on facts and circumstances. Clearly, however, unavailability of *Kovel* engagement data to others in the same office not directly involved in the *Kovel* engagement would be a minimum requirement.

In the case of a corporation, outside or in-house counsel, not corporate management, should hire the forensic accountant. Given the higher standard applied to in-house counsel to trigger application of the attorney-client privilege, any and all steps or procedures that delineate between business and legal advice should be employed by the corporate client.

Next, the attorney should document the relationship with the forensic accountant using a written engagement agreement that defines precisely the terms of the arrangement. The engagement agreement should set forth the legal purpose of the forensic accounting services (Segal 1997). The importance of this agreement is underscored by the *Adlman* decision. If appropriate, the engagement agreement should state that the forensic accountant is being hired in anticipation of litigation. It may also be worthwhile for the attorney to identify in the retainer agreement with the client the likelihood of hiring one or more consultants or experts.

The engagement agreement should also state that all communications among the attorney, client, and forensic accountant are incidental to rendering legal services and are intended to remain confidential (Tigue, Skarlatos, and Lacewell 1994). *Kovel* indicates that the forensic accountant and client may communicate outside the attorney's presence as long as they do so at counsel's direction. The guidance of counsel is critical because in *U.S. v. Bein*,[28] a federal appeals court held that attorney-client privilege did not cover a conversation between an accountant and client outside the presence of the client's attorney despite that the conversation dealt with the client's liability. In the case of a corporation, a written directive from top management or a board resolution should indicate that any communications between employees and agents and the attorney or consultants hired by the attorney are made at the direction of top management. Moreover, none of the parties should disclose the nature or content of any communications or work product to any third party, including government officials, lest the privilege be waived.

In *U.S. v. South Chicago Bank*,[29] the law firm of Winston & Strawn submitted a report to the Illinois Commissioner of Banks & Trusts, at the latter's request. The report was based primarily on a fraud audit of a bank conducted by Coopers & Lybrand, who had been hired by the law firm. A federal district court held that the attorney-client privilege had been waived even though the report was not disclosed voluntarily.

The attorney-forensic accountant engagement agreement should state that all documents, including workpapers, are the property of the lawyer and are to be returned at the lawyer's request (Tigue, Skarlatos, and Lacewell 1994). Any work product prepared by the forensic accountant should be furnished directly to counsel and not the client.

Documents produced by the forensic accountant should be labeled "protected by the attorney-client and work-product privileges" (Twardy and Considine 1996). Any written work product should clearly state that it is being produced pursuant to requests of [the law firm's or corporate legal department's name] (Riback 1999).

Finally, the forensic accountant should directly bill the law firm for whom he works. Neither invoices nor copies of any invoices should be sent to the law firm's client. Payments to the forensic accounting firm should be made by the law firm. The law firm's invoice(s) sent to the client should separately itemize the forensic accountant's fees as expenses (Twardy and Considine 1996).

---

[28] 728 F.2d 107 (2d Cir. 1984).
[9] 1998 U.S. Dist. Lexis 17445 (N.D. Ill. 1998).

ELECTRONIC COMMUNICATIONS AND THE ATTORNEY-CLIENT PRIVILEGE

Forensic accountants (and attorneys) should also be aware of the risks posed to the attorney-client privilege by the use of electronic communications. The widespread use of e-mail, faxes, and cellular telephones has created new opportunities for eavesdropping and inadvertent disclosure of privileged information. Inadvertent disclosure can take many forms, ranging from unintentionally faxing a document to an opposing attorney to the employment of sophisticated espionage methods by adversarial parties (Freeman 1999). Although this is a very unsettled area of the law, in some instances, inadvertent disclosure leads to the waiver of the attorney-client privilege (Gruber 1998). Table 2 contains some recommended safeguards involving electronic communications to preserve the Kovel privilege.

In *U.S. v. Keystone Sanitation*,[30] a federal district court found that the attorney-client privilege had been waived by the inadvertent disclosure of an e-mail sent over a public e-mail system. The court did not specifically consider the e-mail security issue but considered five factors to determine whether the privilege is waived: (1) the reasonableness of the precautions taken to prevent inadvertent disclosure in view of the extent of document production (in the case); (2) the number of inadvertent disclosures; (3) the measures taken to rectify the disclosure; (4) any delay in measures taken to rectify the disclosure; and (5) whether the overriding interests of justice would or would not be served by relieving a party of its error. State and federal courts have not, however, provided consistent, clear rulings in this area.

Some courts will likely require parties to take precautionary measures in using e-mail to be protected by the attorney-client privilege. Reasonable precautions include the use of encryption, internal only e-mail, or secured external systems (Gruber 1998). One legal commentator has suggested that a failure to encrypt an e-mail message may constitute professional negligence on the part of counsel due to a court's finding of waiver of the attorney-client privilege (Froomkin 1995). Thus, forensic accountants

---

[30] 885 F. Supp. 672 (M.D. Pa. 1994).

would be well-advised to avoid sending data, documents, or communications via unencrypted e-mail over the Internet given the potential legal exposure involved.

The use of cellular telephones has also raised questions concerning the attorney-client privilege. Some state bar associations advise against the use of cellular telephones for privileged matters. The reason is that some courts have held there is no reasonable expectation of privacy when utilizing mobile communications (Gruber 1998). Although it is a federal crime to intercept cellular telephone calls under the Electronic Communications Privacy Act of 1986,[31] such a prohibition may not be enough to protect privileged material intercepted by a hacker (Gruber 1998). Forensic accountants need to exercise caution when using cellular

---

[31] 18 U.S.C. §2510 et seq. (1999).

Table 2. Recommended Safeguards for Electronic Communications to Preserve the *Kovel* Privilege

Concern/Safeguard	Description/Reason
Inadvertent disclosure of privileged information through the use of e-mail, faxes, and cell phones can result in the waiver of the attorney-client privilege.	This is a very unsettled area of the law. Five factors considered by some courts to determine whether a privilege is waived by inadvertent disclosure are: 1. reasonableness of precautions taken to prevent disclosure; 2. number of inadvertent disclosures; 3. measures taken to rectify the disclosure; 4. any delay in measures taken to rectify the disclosures; and 5. whether justice could be served by relieving a party of its error.
Some courts may require parties to take precautionary measures in using e-mail to be protected by the attorney-client privilege. Reasonable precautions include the use of encryption, internal only e-mail, or secured external systems.	Given legal uncertainty in this area, forensic accountants may be well-advised to avoid sending data, documents, or communications via unencrypted e-mail.
Some state bar associations advise against the use of cellular phones for privileged matters. Forensic accountants should not discuss or communicate any privileged matters through the use of a cell phone.	Some courts have held there is no reasonable expectation of privacy when utilizing mobile communications.
Waiver of attorney-client privilege by inadvertent disclosure of privileged matter using a fax machine is an unsettled area of the law.	One court applied the five factor test noted above. The most significant factor in the court's opinion is the interests of justice.
Forensic accountants should use fax cover sheets containing a confidential legend every time a fax is sent containing privileged matter.	Such a practice will raise the probability that a court will decide against a waiver of the attorney-client privilege in the event of an inadvertent disclosure.

telephones to protect against waiver of the attorney-client privilege. Standard hard-wire telephones are obligatory when communicating confidential information.

The use of fax machines also represents a new area of inquiry with regard to attorney-client privilege and remains a very unsettled area of the law. In a recent case, however, *Sampson Fire Sales, Inc. v. Jerrell Oaks*,[32] a federal district court addressed the issue of whether attorney-client privilege is waived when a fax was inadvertently sent by the plaintiff's attorney to the defendant. The court applied the five-factor test from *Keystone Sanitation* (noted above) in a step-by-step manner. In the eyes of the court, the most significant factor in the analysis involved the interests of justice. In noting the lack of legal principles or ethical and professional rules on inadvertent disclosure, the court decided that defendant's attorney should have notified the plaintiff's lawyer about the incorrectly sent fax and abided by the cover sheet instructions which stated that the contents were privileged and confidential material. The plaintiff and his attorney were found not to have waived attorney-client privilege.

Accordingly, forensic accountants should make it a practice to use cover sheets containing confidential legends every time a fax is sent containing privileged information. Such a practice will increase the likelihood that a court will decide against a waiver of the attorney-client privilege in the event of the inadvertent disclosure of confidential material.

CONCLUSION

Forensic accountants are frequently hired by clients as non-testifying experts or consultants. The ability to deliver quality services requires the ability to protect communications and work product from disclosure.

---

[32] 201 F.R.D. 351 (M.D. Pa. 2001). When plaintiff sold his business to the defendant, the facility and equipment formerly owned by the plaintiff, including the business telephone and fax number, were used by the defendant as successor owners. Plaintiff's counsel inadvertently sent a one page fax with a cover sheet (which noted that the material was privileged and confidential) to the fax number, believing his client was still in possession of the fax number in Williamsport, Pennsylvania, when, in fact, the fax number forwarded all communications to the defendant in Alabama.

Although some states recognize an accountant-client privilege, such recognition is of dubious value because it is not applicable in federal cases. Federal common law does not recognize an accountant-client privilege. Forensic accountants also cannot protect their work under a work product privilege.

A lawyer may shield a non-testifying forensic accountant under the *Kovel* rule, however, with the attorney-client privilege. This rule insulates forensic accountant-attorney-client communications and work product when the forensic accountant is hired by an attorney to help provide legal services. The privilege extends only to specific communications and not facts. It is critical to the privilege that the communication be made in confidence for the purpose of obtaining legal advice from the attorney. The privilege may be waived unless it is claimed before any disclosure of the communication sought to be protected. Also, the party claiming the privilege bears the burden of proving the existence of the various factors required to sustain it.

A carelessly structured *Kovel* arrangement leaves the attorney-client privilege susceptible to challenge. Various protective measures are vital to preserve the extension of the privilege to forensic accountants. The attorney should hire the forensic accountant under a written engagement agreement that precisely states the terms of the arrangement. The agreement should state the legal purpose of the forensic accounting services. Moreover, the engagement agreement should indicate that all communications among the attorney, client and forensic accountant are to remain confidential and that all workpapers are the lawyer's property.

Forensic accountants and attorneys should be concerned about the risks of inadvertent disclosure and eavesdropping from the use of e-mail, cellular telephones, and faxes. In some cases, inadvertent disclosure leads to the loss of the attorney-client privilege. Unencrypted e-mail of confidential communications should not be sent over the Internet. Cellular telephones should not be used to discuss privileged information. Also, privileged information sent by fax should be transmitted using a cover sheet which states that all material is privileged and confidential.

REFERENCES

Causey, D.Y. and S. Causey. 1999. Duties and Liabilities of Public Accountants. Starkville, MS.: *Accountant's Press*.

Corcoran, A. 2000. The accountant-client privilege: A prescription for confidentiality or just a placebo? *New England Law Review* 34 (Spring): 697-737.

Freeman, E. 1999. Attorney-client privilege and electronic data transmission. *Information Systems Security* 7 (Winter): 46-52.

Froomkin, M. 1995. The metaphor is the key: Cryptography, the clipper chip, and the constitution. *University of Pennsylvania Law Review* 143: 709-897.

Gruber, H. 1998. E-mail: The attorney-client privilege. *George Washington Law Review* 66 (March): 624-656.

Hill, A. 1995. A problem of privilege: In-house counsel and the attorney-client privilege in the united states and the european community. *Case Western Reserve Journal of International Law* 27 (1): 145-195.

Jones, E. 1998. Keeping client confidences: Attorney-client privilege and work-product doctrine in light of *U.S. v. Adlman*. *Pace Law Review* 18 (Spring): 420-471.

LeBlanc, T. 1999. Accountant-client privilege: The effect of the IRS restructuring and reform act of 1998. *University of Missouri at Kansas City Law Review* 67 (Spring): 583-596.

Molony, T. 1998. Is the supreme court ready to recognize another privilege? An examination of the accountant-client privilege in the aftermath of Jaffee v. Redmond. *Washington and Lee Law Review* 55 (Spring): 247-286.

Petroni, A. 1999. Unpacking the accountant-client privilege under IRC section 7525. *Virginia Tax Review* 18 (Spring): 843-874.

Raby, W. and D. Raby. 1995. The Kovel rule and cpa privilege. *Tax Notes* 69 (November): 1125-6.

Riback, S. 1999. Protecting communications: When attorneys and non-legal professionals talk. *New York Law Journal* (10 May): 51.

Segal, M. 1997. Accountants and the attorney-client privilege. *Journal of Accountancy* 181 (April): 53-6.

Sexton, J. 1982. A post-Upjohn consideration of the attorney-client privilege. *New York University Law Review* 57: 443-490.

Spiro, E. and C. Rule. 1994. Kovel experts cloaked by attorney-client privilege: But lawyers must be wary of pitfalls in using consultants. *New York Law Journal* (22 February), S1.

Tigue, J., B. Skarlatos, and L. Lacewell. 1994. The Kovel accountant privilege. *New York Law Journal* (19 May): 3.

Twardy, S. and M. Considine. 1996. Procedures to protect attorney-client privilege. *New York Law Journal* (1 February): 1.

CHAPTER 12

Disentangling *Daubert*: An Epistemological Study in Theory and Practice

Susan Haack

Sometimes the word ["science"] degenerates into a vague honorific, synonymous with the advertiser's "reliable" or "guaranteed"... [JACQUES BARZUN][1]

In *Frye* (1923) the D.C. Court upheld the exclusion of testimony of the results of a then-new blood-pressure deception test on the grounds that novel scientific testimony "crosses the line between the experimental and the demonstrable," and so is admissible, only if it is "sufficiently established to have gained general acceptance in the particular field to which it belongs."[2] Ignored for a decade, rarely cited for a quarter-century, over time the "*Frye* test" became increasingly influential, until by the early 1980s it had been adopted by 29 states.

In 1975, however, newly-enacted Federal Rules of Evidence had set a seemingly less restrictive standard: the testimony of a qualified expert, including a scientific expert, is admissible provided it is relevant (unless it is excluded, under Rule 403, on grounds of unfair prejudice, waste of time,

---

[1] Jacques Barzun, *Science: The Glorious Entertainment* (1964) at 14.

[2] *Frye v. United States*, 54 App.D.C. 46, 293 F. 1013 at 1014.

Susan Haack is Cooper Senior Scholar in Arts and Sciences, Professor of Philosophy, and Professor of Law at the University of Miami. This paper is abridged from "Trial and Error: The Supreme Court's Philosophy of Science," forthcoming in *Am. J. Pub. Health*. It originally appeared in *The American Philosophical Association Newsletter* as "Philosophy and Law", 03.1, Fall 2003, 118-22. Copyright 2003 The American Philosophical Association. Reprinted with permission.

or confusing or misleading the jury). In *Barefoot*, a 1983 constitutional case, the Supreme Court affirmed that the rights of a Texas defendant were not violated by the jury's being allowed to hear psychiatric testimony of his future dangerousness at the sentencing hearing — even though an amicus brief from the American Psychiatric Association reported that 2 out of 3 such predictions are mistaken. Writing for the majority, Justice White observed that state and federal rules of evidence "anticipate that relevant, unprivileged testimony should be admitted and its weight left to the fact-finder, who would have the benefit of cross-examination and contrary evidence by the opposing party."[3] Justice Blackmun wrote an angry dissent.

In 1991, amid increasing public concern that the tort system was getting out of hand, Peter Huber argued in his influential *Galileo's Revenge* that under the Federal Rules worthless "junk science," which would have been excluded by the *Frye* test, was flooding the courts. In 1992 proposals to tighten up the Federal Rules were before Congress. In 1993 the Supreme Court issued its ruling in *Daubert*[4] – the first case in its 204-year history where the central questions concerned the admissibility of scientific testimony. The *Frye* rule arose in a criminal case, and had for most of its history been cited in criminal cases; but *Daubert* was a tort action in which the trial court had relied on *Frye* in excluding the plaintiffs' experts' testimony that the morning-sickness drug Bendectin was teratogenic. So the Supreme Court was to determine whether the FRE had superseded *Frye*, and in particular how Rule 702 was to be interpreted.

Yes, Justice Blackmun wrote for the unamious court, the FRE had superseded *Frye*; but the Rules themselves require judges to screen proffered expert testimony not only for relevance, but also for reliability. In doing this, he continues (in a part of the ruling from which Justice Rehnquist and Justice Stevens disented) courts must look, not to an expert's conclusions, but to his "methodology," to determine whether proffered evidence is really "scientific ... knowledge," and hence reliable. As to what that methodology is, citing an article by law professor Michael Green citing Karl Popper, and quoting an observation of Carl Hempel's for good measure, the *Daubert* ruling suggests four factors that courts might use in assessing reliability: "falsifiability," i.e., whether proffered evidence "can be and has

---

[3] *Barefoot v. Estelle*, 463 U.S. 880 at 898, 103 S.Ct. 3383 (1983) at 3397. Mr. Barefoot was executed in 1984.

[4] *Daubert v. Merrell Dow Pharm., Inc.*, 509 U.S. 579, 113 S.Ct. 2786 (1993.)

been tested;" the known or potential error rate; peer review and publication; and (in a nod to *Frye*), acceptance in the relevant community.[5]

In partial dissent, however, pointing out that the word "reliable" nowhere occurs in the text of Rule 702, Justice Rehnquist anticipated difficulties over whether and if so how *Daubert* should be applied to non-scientific expert testimony; worried aloud that federal judges were being asked to become amateur scientists; and questioned the wisdom of his colleagues' readiness to get involved in philosophy of science. I think he was right to suspect that something was seriously amiss; in fact, what I shall have to say here might be read as an exploration, amplification, and partial defense of his reservations about that philosophical excursus.

– – *** – –

Apparently equating the question of whether expert testimony is reliable with the question of whether it is genuinely scientific, taking for granted that there is some scientific "methodology" which, faithfully followed, guarantees reliable results, and casting about for a philosophy of science to fit this demanding bill, the *Daubert* Court settled on an unstable amalgam of Popper's and Hempel's very different approaches – neither of which, however, is suitable to the task at hand.

Popper describes his philosophy of science as "Falsificationist," by contrast with the Verificationism of the Logical Positivists, because his key theme is that scientific statements can never be shown conclusively to be true, but can sometimes be shown conclusively to be false. Hence his criterion of demarcation: to be genuinely scientific, a statement must be "testable" – meaning, in Popper's mouth, "refutable" or "falsifiable," i.e., susceptible to evidence that could potentially show it to be false (if it is false). Curiously, Popper acknowledged from the beginning that his criterion of demarcation is a "convention;" and in 1959, in his Introduction to the English edition of *The Logic of Scientific Discovery*, affirmed that scientific knowledge is continuous with common-sense knowledge.[6] Nevertheless, his

---

[5] The *Daubert* Court did not itself scrutinize the disputed testimony; on remand, Judge Kozinski again excluded the plaintiffs' proffered experts, this time under *Daubert* rather than *Frye*. Because of litigation costs, Merrell Dow had already taken Bendectin off the market in 1984. In 2000 the FDA again declared the drug safe.

[6] Karl R. Popper, *The Logic of Scientific Discovery* (1934), 37; Preface, 1959 to the English edition of this book, 18.

whole philosophy of science turns on his criterion of demarcation. Falsifiability is to discriminate real empirical science, such as Einstein's theory
of relativity, from pre-scientific myths, from non-empirical disciplines like
pure mathematics or metaphysics, from non-scientific disciplines like history, and from such pseudo-sciences as Freud's and Adler's psychoanalytic
theories and Marx's "scientific socialism."[7] Falsifiability is also central to
Popper's account of the method of science as "conjecture and refutation":
making a bold, highly falsifiable guess, testing it as severely as possible,
and, if it is found to be false, giving it up and starting over rather than
protecting it by ad hoc or "conventionalist" modifications. (This readiness
to accept falsification and eschew ad hoc stratagems is Popper's "methodological criterion" of the genuinely scientific.)

Popper also describes his philosophy of science as "Deductivist," by contrast with "Inductivism," whether in the strong, Baconian form that posits
an inductive logic for arriving at hypotheses or in the weaker, Logical
Positivist form that posits an inductive logic of confirmation. According to
Popper, Hume showed long ago that induction is unjustifiable. But science
doesn't need induction; the method of conjecture and refutation requires
only deductive logic – specifically, *modus tollens*, the rule invoked when
an observational result predicted by a theory fails.

Theories which have been tested but not yet falsified are "corroborated,"
the degree of corroboration at a time depending on the number and sever-
ity of the tests passed. That a theory is corroborated, to however high a
degree, doesn't show that it is true, or even probable; indeed, the degree
of testability of a hypothesis is inversely related to its degree of logical
probability.[8] Corroboration is not a measure of verisimilitude, but at best
an indicator of how the verisimilitude of a theory *appears*, relative to
other theories, at a time;[9] and that a theory is corroborated doesn't mean
that it is rational to believe it. (It does mean, Popper writes, that it is rational to prefer the theory as the basis for practical action; not, however, that
there are good reasons for thinking the theory will be successful in future

[7] See Karl R. Popper, Philosophy of Science: A Personal Report, in *British Philosophy in
Mid-Century* (C.A. Mace. ed., 1957), reprinted in Karl R. Popper, *Conjectures And
Refutations: The Growth Of Scientific Knowledge* (1962), 33, and in *Scientific Inquiry*
(Robert Klee, ed., 1999), 65; and The Problem of Demarcation (1974; reprinted in *A
Pocket Popper* (David Miller, ed., 1983), 118.

[8] Karl R. Popper, *The Logic Of Scientific Discovery* (Supra, Note 7), Section 83.

[9] Karl R. Popper, *Objective Knowledge: An Evolutionary Approach* (1972), 102.

— *there can be* no good reasons for believing this.[10] So it seems that all this "concession" amounts to is that in deciding how to act we can do no better than go with theories we don't so far know to be false.)

The first problem with the *Daubert* Court's reliance on Popper is that applying his criterion of demarcation is no trivial matter; as Justice Rehnquist pointed out, observing wryly that, since he didn't really know what is meant by saying that a theory is "falsifiable," he doubted federal judges would, either.[11] Indeed, Popper himself doesn't seem quite sure how to apply his criterion. Sometimes, for example, he says that the theory of evolution is not falsifiable, and so is not science; at one point he suggests that "survival of the fittest" is a tautology, or "near-tautology," and elsewhere that evolution is really a historical theory, or perhaps metaphysics. Then he changes his mind: evolution is science, after all.[12] It's ironic; for Popper's criterion of demarcation had already found its way into the U.S. legal system, a decade before *Daubert*, in a 1982 first-amendment case: *McLean v. Arkansas Board of Education*, where Michael Ruse's testimony that creation science is not science, by Popper's criterion, but the theory of evolution is, apparently persuaded Judge Overton.[13]

But there is an even more serious problem with the *Daubert* Court's reliance on Popper, of which Justice Rehnquist doesn't seem aware: Popper's philosophy of science is signally inappropriate to the Court's concern with reliability. When Popper describes his approach as "Critical Rationalism," it is to emphasize that the rationality of the scientific enterprise lies in the susceptibility of scientific theories to criticism, i.e., to testing, and potentially to falsification, not in their verifiability or confirmability.

---

[10] Id. at 22.

[11] *Daubert*, 509 U.S. 579 at 600, 113 S.Ct. 2786 at 2800. Some federal judges evidently understand falsifiability better than others. In *U.S. v. Havvard*, 117 F.Supp. 2d 848, 854, admitting fingerprint identification testimony, Judge Hamilton observes that "the methods of latent print identification ... have been tested ... for roughly 100 years ... in adversarial proceedings." But in Llera-Plaza I, 2002 WL 27305 (E.D.Pa, Jan 2, 2002), 273 10, imposing restrictions on fingerprint identification testimony, Judge Pollak points out that "'adversarial' testing in court is not ... what the Supreme Court meant when it discussed testing as an admissibility factor."

[12] See K. R. Popper, Natural Selection and Its Scientific Status (excerpted from a lecture of 1977, in *A Pocket Popper* (supra, note 8)) at 298.

[13] *McLean v. Arkansas Board of Education*, 529 F.Supp. 1255 (1982). Judge Overton's ruling, and Ruse's testimony, along with Larry Laudan's properly scathing critique, can be found in *But Is It Science? The Philosophical Question In The Creation/Evolution Controversy* (Michael Ruse, ed. 1996).

True, early on Carnap translated Popper's word *"Bewährung"* by "confirmation;" and for a while, thinking the issue merely verbal, Popper let it go – even, occasionally, using "confirm" himself. But in a footnote to the English edition of *The Logic of Scientific Discovery* he comments that this had been a bad mistake on his part, conveying the false impression that a theory's having been corroborated means that it is probably true.[14] Except for the weak moments when he condoned Carnap's (mis)translation, Popper insisted that corroboration must not be confused with confirmation.

The degree of corroboration of a theory represents its past performance only, and *"says nothing whatever about future performance, or about the 'reliability' of a theory;"* even the best-tested theory "is not 'reliable'"[15] – so scornful is Popper of the concept of reliability that he refuses even to use the word without putting it in precautionary scare quotes! Reiterating that he puts the emphasis "on *negative arguments*, such as negative instances or counter-examples, refutations, and attempted refutations – in short, criticism – while the inductivist lays stress on *'positive instances,'* from which he draws 'non-demonstrative *inferences,'* and which he hopes will guarantee the *'reliability'* of the conclusions of these inferences," Popper specifically identifies Hempel as representative of those inductivists with whom he disagrees.[16]

Hempel is not, perhaps, the prototypical inductivist: he describes the method of science as "hypothetico-deductive;" he affirms that scientific claims should be subject to empirical check or testing; and he doesn't follow Reichenbach and Carnap in explaining confirmation by appeal to the calculus of probabilities. Nevertheless, Popper is surely right to see Hempel's approach as very significantly at odds with his own: Hempel is not centrally concerned with demarcating science; he questions the supposed asymmetry between verification and falsification, and argues that Popper's criterion "involves a very severe restriction of the possible forms

---

[14] Karl R. Popper, *The Logic of Scientific Discovery* (supra, note 7), 251-2, note *1, added in the English edition. When Popper uses "confirm" for "corroborate" – as he does in his 1957 *Philosophy of Science: A Personal Report* (supra, note 8) – the effect is powerfully confusing.

[15] Karl R. Popper, *Objective Knowledge* (supra, note 10) 18, 22.

[16] Id. at 20; the reference to Hempel is in footnote 29.

of scientific hypotheses," e.g., in ruling out purely existential statements;[17] when he speaks of "testing" he envisages both disconfirmation and confirmation of a hypothesis; and one of his chief projects was to articulate the "logic of confirmation," i.e., of the support of general hypotheses by positive instances.

Apparently the Supreme Court hoped, by combining Hempel's account of confirmation with Popper's criterion of demarcation, to craft a crisp test to identify genuine, and hence reliable, science. But, though Hempel's philosophy of science is more positive than Popper's, it isn't much more help with the question of reliability. For one thing, the confirmation of generalizations by positive instances which preoccupies Hempel is just too simplified to apply to the enormously complex congeries of epidemiological, toxicological, etc., etc., evidence at stake in a case like *Daubert*. For another, Hempel himself seems eventually to have concluded (rightly, I believe) that the "grue" paradox shows that confirmation isn't a purely syntactic or logical notion after all,[18] and late in life began to think that maybe Kuhn had been on the right track.[19]

But the most fundamental problem is that what Hempel offered was an account of supportiveness of evidence, or as he said, of "relative confirmation," the relation between observational evidence and hypothesis, expressible as "E confirms H [to degree n]," or "H is confirmed [to degree n] by evidence E." This, as Hempel acknowledged, falls short of an account of "absolute confirmation," the warrant of a scientific claim, which would be expressed in non-relative terms, as "H is confirmed [to degree n], period." To discriminate reliable testimony from unreliable, however, would require an account of the non-relative concept – which Hempel doesn't supply.

---

[17] Carl G. Hempel, Studies in the Logic of Confirmation, 54 *Mind* 1-26 and 97-121 (1945), reprinted in Carl G. Hempel, *Aspects Of Scientific Explanation And Other Essays In The Philosophy Of Science* (1965), 43-4. See also his Empiricist Criteria of Cognitive Significance: Problems and Changes (adapted from two papers originally published in 1950 and 1951) and Postscript (1964) on Cognitive Significance, 99-122 Aspects Of Scientific Explanation.

[18] Carl G. Hempel, Postscript (1964) on Confirmation, 47 *Aspects Of Scientific Explanation* (supra, note 18), 51.

[19] Carl G. Hempel, The Irrelevance of Truth for the Critical Appraisal of Scientific Theories (1990: reprinted in *Hempel: Selected Philosophical Essays* (Richard Jeffrey, ed., 2000), 75).

− − *** − −

So, the *Daubert* Court mixes up its Hoppers and its Pempels; but isn't this just a slip, of merely scholarly interest? No: it is symptomatic of the serious misunderstanding of the place of the sciences within inquiry generally revealed by the Court's equation of "scientific" and "reliable."

So successful have the natural sciences been that the words "science," "scientific," and "scientifically" are often used as generic terms of epistemological praise, meaning vaguely "strong, reliable, good" – as, in television advertisements, actors in white coats urge viewers to get their clothes cleaner with new, "scientific," Wizzo. This honorific usage is unmistakably at work in the *Daubert* ruling; indeed, it seems to be implicit even in the way Justice Blackmun writes of "scientific ... knowledge," strategically excising a significant phrase from the reference in FRE 702 to "scientific or other technical knowledge," and apparently signalling an expectation that a criterion of the genuinely scientific will also discriminate reliable testimony from unreliable.

If "scientific" is used honorifically, it is a tautology that "scientific" = "reliable;" but this tautology, obviously, is of no help to a judge trying to screen proffered scientific testimony. If "scientific" is used descriptively, however, "scientific" and "reliable" come apart: for, obviously, physicists, chemists, biologists, medical scientists, etc., are sometimes incompetent, confused, self-deceived, dishonest, or simply mistaken, while historians, detectives, investigative journalists, legal and literary scholars, plumbers, auto mechanics, etc., are sometimes good investigators. In short, not all, and not only, scientists are reliable inquirers; and not all, and not only, scientific evidence is reliable. Nor is there a "scientific method" in the sense the Court assumed: no uniquely rational mode of inference or procedure of inquiry used by all scientists and only by scientists. Rather, as Einstein once put it, scientific inquiry is "nothing but a refinement of our everyday thinking,"[20] superimposing on the inferences, desiderata, and constraints common to all serious investigation a vast variety of constantly evolving local ways and means of stretching the imagination, amplifying reasoning power, extending evidential reach, and stiffening respect for evidence.

---

[20] Albert Einstein, Physics and Reality (1936), in *Ideas And Opinions Of Albert Einstein* (Sonja Bargmann, trans., 1954), 290.

Every kind of empirical inquiry, from the simplest everyday puzzling over the causes of delayed buses or spoiled food to the most complex investigations of detectives, of historians, of legal and literary scholars, and of scientists, involves making an informed guess about the explanation of some event or phenomenon, figuring out the consequences of its being true, and checking how well those consequences stand up to evidence. This is the procedure of all scientists; but it is not the procedure only of scientists. Something like the "hypothetico-deductive method," really is the core of all inquiry, scientific inquiry included. But it is not distinctive of scientific inquiry; and the fact that scientists, like inquirers of every kind, proceed in this way tells us nothing substantive about whether or when their testimony is reliable.

The sciences have extended the senses with specialized instruments; stretched the imagination with metaphors, analogies, and models; amplified reasoning power with numerals, the calculus, computers; and evolved a social organization that enables cooperation, competition, and evidence-sharing, allowing each scientist to take up his investigation where others left off. Astronomers devise ever more sophisticated telescopes, chemists ever more sophisticated techniques of analysis, medical scientists ever more sophisticated methods of imaging bodily states and processes, and so on; scientists work out what controls are needed to block a potential source of experimental error, what statistical techniques to rule out a merely coincidental correlation, and so forth. But these scientific "helps" to inquiry are local and evolving, not used by all scientists.[21]

You may object that, since I have acknowledged that scientific inquiry is continuous with everyday empirical inquiry, I have in effect agreed with Popper that science is an extension of common sense. Indeed, I think science is well-described, in Gustav Bergmann's wonderfully evocative phrase, as the Long Arm of Common Sense. But the continuity is not between the content of scientific and of common-sense knowledge, but between the basic ways and means of everyday and of scientific inquiry; and it is precisely because of this continuity that the Popperian preoccupation with the "problem of demarcation" is a distraction.

---

[21] For a detailed development of the conception of scientific method on which I have relied here, see Susan Haack, *Defending Science – Within Reason: Between Scientism And Cynicism* (2003), chapter 4.

Or you may object that the *Daubert* Court's Popperian advice that courts ask whether proffered scientific testimony "can be and has been tested" surely is potentially helpful. This is true; but it is no real objection. "Check whether proffered testimony has been tested" is very good advice when a purported expert hasn't made even the most elementary effort to check how well his claims stand up to evidence: such as the knife-mark examiner in *Ramirez*,[22] who testified that he could infallibly identify this knife, to the exclusion of all other knives in the world, as having made the wound – though no study had established the assumed uniqueness of individual knives, and his purported ability to make such infallible identifications was untested. This is not, however, because falsifiability is the criterion of the scientific, but because any serious inquirer is required to seek out all the potentially available evidence, and to go where it leads, even if he would prefer to avoid, ignore, or play down information that pulls against what he hopes is true.

Yes, this is a requirement on scientists; as Darwin recognized when he wrote in his autobiography that he always made a point of recording recalcitrant examples and contrary arguments in a special notebook, to safeguard against his tendency conveniently to forget negative evidence.[23] But it is no less a requirement on other inquirers, too; as we all realized a few years ago, when a historian who announced that he had evidence that Marilyn Monroe had blackmailed President Kennedy turned out to have ignored the fact that the supposedly incriminating letters were typed with correction ribbon, and that the address included a zip code – when neither existed at the time the letters were purportedly written![24]

"Non-science" is an ample and diverse category, including the many human activities other than inquiry, the various forms of pseudo-inquiry, inquiry of a non-empirical character, and empirical inquiry of other kinds than the scientific; and of course there are plenty of mixed and borderline cases. The honorific use of "science" and its cognates tempts us – like the *Daubert* Court – to criticize poorly-conducted science as not really sci-

---

[22] *Ramirez v. State,* 542 So. 2d 352 (Fla. 1989); *Ramirez v. State,* 651 So. 2d 1164 (Fla. 1995); *Ramirez v. State,* 8120 So. 2d 836 (Fla. 2001). Florida remains officially a *Frye* state, but seems to be rapidly evolving in the direction of (as Michael Saks puts it) *Fryebert.*

[23] Charles Darwin, *Autobiography And Letters* (Francis Darwin, ed., 1893), 45.

[24] See Evan Thomas, Mark Hosenball, and Michael Isikoff, The JFK-Marilyn Hoax, *Newsweek,* June 6, 1997, 36-7.

ence at all; but "not scientific" is as unhelpful as generic epistemic criticism as "scientific" is as generic epistemic praise. The pejorative tone of the phrase "pseudo-science," which presumably refers to activities which purport to be science but aren't really, derives in part from its imputation of false pretenses, and in part from the favorable connotations of "scientific." But rather than sneering unhelpfully that this or that work is "pseudo-scientific," it is always better to specify what, exactly, is wrong with it: that it is not honestly or seriously conducted; that it rests on vague or flimsy assumptions – assumptions there is no way to check, or for which there is no good evidence; that it seeks to impress with decorative or distracting mathematical symbolism or elaborate-looking apparatus; that it fails to take essential precautions against experimental error; or whatever.

– – *** – –

So, the *Daubert* Court's philosophy of science was muddled; but haven't subsequent Supreme Court rulings cleared things up? Not exactly: it would be more accurate to say that in *Joiner* (1997) and *Kumho* (1999) the Supreme Court quietly backed away from *Daubert's* confused philosophy of science.[25] At any rate, those references to Hepper, Pompel, falsifiability etc., so prominent in *Daubert*, are conspicuous by their absence from Joiner and Kumho. But there are points of epistemological interest.

In *Joiner* there is a bit of a kerfuffle about "methodology:" Mr. Joiner's attorneys had argued that the lower court erred in excluding their proffered expert testimony because, instead of focusing exclusively on their experts' methodology – which, they maintain, was the very same "weight of evidence" methodology used by the other party's (G.E.'s) experts – it improperly concerned itself with the experts' conclusions. Apparently anxious to sidestep this argument, the *Joiner* Court (with the exception of Justice Stevens) flatly denies the legitimacy of the distinction between methodology and conclusions. Opining that this is No Real Distinction, the Court sounds like nothing so much as a conclave of medieval logicians; but given their citation to *Paoli*,[26] it seems likely that they didn't really intend to make a profound metaphysical pronouncement, only to

---

[25] *General Electric Co. v. Joiner*, 522 U.S. 136, 118 S.Ct. 512 (1997); *Kumho Tire Co. v. Carmichael*, 526 U.S. 137, 119 S.Ct. 1167 (1999).

[26] *In re. Paoli R.R. Yard PCB Litig.*, 35 F.3d. 717 (3d Cir. 1994).

acknowledge, as Judge Becker had, that if an expert's conclusions are problematic enough, this alerts us to the possibility of some methodological defect.

This focus on "methodology" – an accordion concept expanded and contracted as the argument demands[27] – obscured a much deeper epistemological question. Mr. Joiner's attorneys proffered a collage of bits of information, none sufficient by itself to warrant the conclusion that exposure to PCBs promoted Mr. Joiner's cancer, but which, they argued, taken together gave strong support to that conclusion; G.E.'s attorneys replied, in effect, that piling up weak evidence can't magically transform it into strong evidence. In response, Mr. Joiner's attorneys refer to the EPA guidelines for assessing the combined weight of epidemiological, toxicological, etc., evidence. But no-one ever addresses the key question: is there a difference between a congeries of evidence so interrelated that the whole really is greater than the sum of its parts, and a collection of unrelated and insignificant bits of information, between true consilience and the "faggot fallacy"[28] – and if so, what is it?

There is a difference. Evidence of means, motive, and opportunity may interlock to support the claim that the defendant did it much more strongly than any of these pieces of evidence alone could do. Similarly, evidence of increased incidence of a disease among people exposed to a suspected substance may interlock with evidence that animals biologically similar to humans are harmed by exposure to that substance, and evidence indicating what chemical mechanism may be responsible, to support the claim that this substance causes, promotes, or contributes to the disease much more strongly than any of these pieces of evidence alone could do. However, the interlocking will be less robust if, e.g., the animals are unlike humans in some relevant way, or if the mechanism postulated to cause damage is also present in other chemicals not found to be associated with an increased risk of disease, or, etc.

---

[27] The term "accordion concept" was introduced in Wilfrid Sellars, Scientific Realism or Irenic Instrumentalism?, *Boston Studies In The Philosophy Of Science*, 2 (Robert Cohen and Marx Wartofsky, eds., 1965), 172.

[28] The word "consilience," meaning etymologically "jumping together," was coined by William Whewell, and recently made famous as the title of a best-selling book, E. O. Wilson, *Consilience* (1998), on the Unity of Science. The phrase "faggot fallacy" was introduced in Petr Skrabanek and J. Mccormick, *Follies And Fallacies In Medicine* (1997), and adopted by G.E.'s attorneys in *Joiner*.

"Interlocking" is exactly the right word; for evidence is structured like a crossword puzzle, with each claim, anchored by experiential evidence (the analogue of the clues), enmeshed in reasons (the analogue of completed intersecting entries). How reasonable a crossword entry is depends on how well it is supported by the clue and completed intersecting entries, how reasonable those other entries are, independent of this one, and how much of the crossword has been completed; similarly, how warranted a claim is depends on how supportive the evidence is, how secure the reasons are, independent of this claim itself, and how much of the relevant evidence the evidence includes.[29] Because of the ramification of reasons, the desirable kind of interlocking of evidence gestured at in *Joiner* is subtle and complex, not easily captured by any mechanical weighting of epidemiological data relative to animal studies or toxicological evidence. Nor, moreover – as Justice Rehnquist already pointed out in *Daubert* – can its quality readily be judged by someone who lacks the necessary background knowledge.

In *Kumho* the Supreme Court made a real epistemological step forward. In this products-liability case, focused on the proffered testimony of an expert on tire failure, the Court tried to sort out the problems with non-scientific experts which, as Justice Rehnquist had anticipated, soon arose in the wake of *Daubert*; and ruled that judges can't evade their gatekeeping duty on the grounds that proffered expert testimony is not science: the key word in FRE 702, after all, is "knowledge," not "scientific." No longer fussing over demarcation, recognizing the gap between "scientific" and "reliable," in *Kumho* the Supreme Court acknowledges that what matters is whether proffered testimony is reliable, not whether it is scientific. Quite so.

Far from backing away from federal courts' gatekeeping responsibilities, however, the *Joiner* Court had affirmed that a judge's decision to allow or exclude scientific testimony, even though it may be outcome-determinative, is subject only to review for abuse of discretion, not to any more stringent standard; and the *Kumho* Court, pointing out that, depending on the

---

[29] First introduced the analogy in Rebuilding the Ship While Sailing on the Water (in Roger Gibson and Robert Barrett, eds, *Perspectives On Quine*, 1990, 111). It was articulated in more detail in Susan Haack, *Evidence And Inquiry: Towards Reconstruction In Epistemology* (1993), chapter 4, and is developed further in Susan Haack, *Defending Science – Within Reason* (supra, note 22), chapter 3.

nature of the expertise in question, the *Daubert* factors may or may not
be appropriate, held that it is within judges' discretion to use any, all, or
none of them. A year later, revised Federal Rules made explicit what
according to *Daubert* had been implicit in Rule 702 all along: admissible
expert testimony must be based on "sufficient" data, the product of "reliable" testimony "reliably" applied to the facts of the case. Federal judges
now have large responsibilities and broad discretion in screening not only
scientific testimony but expert testimony generally – but very little guidance about how to perform this difficult task.

In short, since *Kumho's* epistemological step forward, the other problem
Justice Rehnquist worried about – that judges generally lack the background knowledge which may be essential to a serious appraisal of the
worth of scientific (or other technical) testimony – is not merely unre-
solved, but more acute than ever. Bad epistemology can only get in the
way; but better epistemology, unfortunately, can't by itself ensure smooth
legal sailing.[30]

---

[30] My thanks to Mark Migotti for very helpful comments on a draft.

CONTRIBUTING AUTHORS

Steven Babitsky, Esq., is President of SEAK, Inc. Mr. Babitsky was a personal injury trial attorney for twenty years and is the former managing partner of the firm Kistin, Babitsky, Latimer & Beitman. Mr. Babitsky is the co-author of the texts *Writing and Defending Your Expert Report: The Step-by-Step Guide with Models*; *How to Excel During Cross-Examination: Techniques for Experts That Work*; *Cross-Examination: The Comprehensive Guide For Experts*; *The Comprehensive Forensic Services Manual: The Essential Resources for All Experts*; *National Guide to Expert Witness Fees and Billing Procedures*; and *How to Excel During Depositions: Techniques for Experts That Work*. Attorney Babitsky is seminar leader for the Annual National Expert Witness and Litigation Conference, and trains hundreds of experts every year.

David Barnhill is an attorney for the Montana Department of Public Health & Human Services, Child Support Enforcement Division, where he serves as an interstate attorney, working on cases originating in other states or foreign nations regarding establishment of paternity and child support orders and their enforcement. He is also a part-time adjunct instructor at the Helena Center of Technology of the University of Montana, where he currently teaches classes in ethics and employment law. Previously, Mr. Barnhill taught numerous courses in business and law at Montana State University in Bozeman, as well as at Carroll College in Helena, Montana. Mr. Barnhill earned his J.D. degree from the University of Montana, and he also holds a B.A. degree in History from the University of Montana, having graduated with honors. Mr. Barnhill has several years of professional legal experience, which includes serving as a county attorney and a city attorney, in addition to experience in private general practice.

Dana Basney, MSBA, CPA, CIRA, CVA is a shareholder in the Certified Public Accounting Firm of Mayer Hoffman McCann P.C., and is a Director of CBIZ Nation Smith Hermes Diamond in San Diego. He is the Director in charge of the San Diego office's due diligence, litigation and insolvency services. Mr. Basney has qualified and testified as an expert witness on numerous occasions in cases involving

181

accounting, valuation and tax matters before the Federal District and Bankruptcy Courts and California Superior Courts. Additionally, Mr. Basney has acted as a consultant to attorneys in both civil and criminal cases in Federal District Court, state courts, and the High Courts of Guam and American Samoa. Mr. Basney has also been appointed as special master, joint expert in matters of valuation and accounting, mediator and settlement referee in a number of court cases. Mr. Basney has taught a variety of accounting and business classes since 1978. Since 1982, he has taught accounting classes through the University of California at San Diego Extension program, including classes in advanced accounting, consolidations, mergers, acquisitions, managerial accounting, financial statement analysis, and the State Board of Accountancy approved Professional Ethics and Conduct for Accountants class. He is a member of the American Institute of Certified Public Accountants, the California Society of Certified Public Accountants, the Institute of Managerial Accountants, the Association of Insolvency Accountants, the Institute of Business Appraisers, Inc., and the Bankruptcy Forum. He has served on the San Diego Family Law Bar's Business Valuation Subcommittee. He has also co-chaired both the Ethics Committee and the Litigation Support Committee for the San Diego Chapter of the California Society Certified Public Accountants.

Thomas A. Buckhoff, Ph.D., CPA, CFE is an Associate Professor of Forensic Accounting at Georgia Southern University. Dr. Buckhoff also works as a senior forensic consultant for Eide Bailly, LLP - Fraudwise Division. Dr. Buckhoff received his Bachelors and Master of Accountancy degrees from Brigham Young University and his Ph.D. in accounting from the University of Kentucky. He is a Certified Public Accountant (CPA) and a Certified Fraud Examiner (CFE). Previously, Dr. Buckhoff worked as a senior forensic accountant for Eide Bailly, LLP - Fraudwise Division, as the Eide Bailly Professor of Forensic Accounting at North Dakota State University, and as an Assistant Professor at the University of Southern Maine. Dr. Buckhoff frequently conducts anti-fraud continuing professional education (CPE) seminars for organizations including the American Institute of Certified Public Accountants, American Accounting Association, Association of Certified Fraud Examiners, state CPA societies, state auditors, CPA Australia, law enforcement agencies, and various *Fortune* 500 companies. Tom has published a variety of anti-fraud articles in the *Journal of Forensic Accounting, Journal of Accountancy, Advances in Accounting Education, Journal of Financial Crime, The CPA Journal, New Accountant, Issues in Accounting Education,* and *The White Paper: Topical Issues in White-Collar Crime.* He is on the editorial board for *The CPA Journal* and served as Associate Editor for the *Journal of Forensic Accounting.*

D. Larry Crumbley, Ph.D., CPA, CFD, CrFA is KPMG endowed Professor of Accounting at Louisiana State University, in Baton Rouge, Louisiana. He is the Editor-in-Chief of the *Journal of Forensic Accounting: Auditing, Fraud and Risk*, former chair of the Executive Board of Forensic Accountants, member of the NACVA's Fraud Deterrence Board, and the AICPA's Fraud Task Force (2003-2004). A frequent contributor to the *Forensic Examiner*, Professor Crumbley is co-author of the CCH *Master Auditing Guide*, along with more than 50 other books and 350 articles. His latest book, entitled *Forensic and Investigative Accounting*, is published by Commerce Clearing House. Some of his 12 educational novels have as the main character a forensic accountant.

Susan Haack, Ph.D. is Cooper Senior Scholar in Arts and Sciences, Professor of Philosophy, and Professor of Law at the University of Miami, Coral Gables, Florida. Dr. Haack is author of *Defending Science - Within Reason: Between Scientism and Cynicism* (2003).

William Hillison, CPA, CMA, is a Professor of Accounting at Florida State University where he teaches courses on auditing and accounting information systems. He has published more than 60 academic and professional articles and co-authors the popular book, *CPA Review - Auditing*, with Irv Gleim.

Bonita K. Peterson Kramer, Ph.D., CPA, CMA, CIA is a Professor of Accounting in the College of Business at Montana State University in Bozeman, where she teaches courses in auditing, financial accounting, and fraud examination. Dr. Peterson is responsible for preparing graduate students for the auditing section of the CPA exam, and for the past three years her graduate auditing students have ranked #3, #1 and #2 in the country for their first-time pass rate on the auditing portion of the exam. In 2003, she was awarded the Montana Society of Certified Public Accountants Jack J. Kempner Outstanding Educator Award. Her research focuses primarily on accounting education and fraud-related topics, and she has published articles in several academic and practitioner journals, including *Behavioral Research in Accounting, Issues in Accounting Education, Journal of Accounting Education, Advances in Accounting Education, Strategic Finance, Journal of Forensic Accounting, Journal of Accountancy, The CPA Journal*, and *Internal Auditor*. She has also co-authored an on-line fraud examination practice set, published in 2004, by Thomson/Southwestern Publishing Company.

James J. Mangraviti, Jr., Esq., has trained hundreds of expert witnesses across the United States and Canada. He is a former trial lawyer with experience in defense and plaintiff personal injury law and insurance law. He currently serves as Vice President and General Counsel of SEAK, Inc. Mr. Mangraviti received his BA degree in mathematics summa cum laude from Boston College and his JD degree cum laude from Boston College Law School. His publications include the texts *Cross-Examination: The Comprehensive Guide For Experts*; *National Guide to Expert Witness Fees and Billing Procedures*; *Writing and Defending Your IME Report*; *The Successful Physician Negotiator: How to Get What You Deserve*; *How to Excel During Cross-Examination: Techniques for Experts That Work*; *How to Excel During Depositions: Techniques for Experts That Work*; *The Comprehensive Forensic Services Manual: The Essential Resources for All Experts*; and *Writing and Defending Your Expert Report: The Step-by-Step Guide with Models*.

William M. Michaelson, CPA, CFE, MAE, DABFA, has provided accounting services for over 28 years throughout the country and internationally. Mr. Michaelson is a graduate of the University of Miami and a Certified Public Accountant in Florida and Tennessee. As president of Michaelson & Co., P.A., an accounting and consulting firm located in West Palm Beach, Florida, Mr. Michaelson has successfully developed expertise in forensic accounting and fraud detection, including serving as an expert witness in court proceedings. He holds the distinction of Certified Fraud Examiner and is a frequent speaker on fraud detection and forensic accounting topics before national, state and local forums. Bill has written articles for publications such as *The Journal of Accountancy*, *The Practical Accountant*, and *Florida CPA Today*, and is a member of the Editorial Board of the *Journal of Forensic Accounting*. He is a member of the American Institute of Certified Public Accountants, Florida Institute of Certified Public Accountants, Florida Advisory Committee on Arson Prevention, and the Academy of Experts, an international professional society and qualifying body for experienced expert witnesses, and is a Diplomat of the American Board of Forensic Accountants.

David Nolte is the founding principal at Fulcrum Financial Inquiry LLP. He has 30 years experience performing forensic accounting, auditing, business appraisals, and related financial consulting. He regularly serves as an expert witness involving accounting, business valuation, finance and economic damages. Mr. Nolte is a Certified Public Accountant (CPA), an Accredited Senior Appraiser (ASA), and a Registered Investment Advisor. The website address of Fulcrum Financial Inquiry LLP is *www.fulcruminquiry.com*.

Carl Pacini is Associate Professor of Accounting and Business Law at Florida Gulf Coast University, where he teaches auditing, forensic accounting, international accounting and business law courses. In his forensic accounting courses, he has worked closely with the FBI and IRS. He also teaches as an Adjunct Professor of Forensic Accounting at Florida Atlantic University in Ft. Lauderdale. He received his Ph.D. in accounting from Florida State University in 1997 and his law degree from the University of Notre Dame in 1979. He is a Florida CPA, a Certified Financial Services Auditor, and a member of the Florida Bar. He has worked as a practicing attorney, internal compliance auditor, and vice president of real estate lending in the banking industry in Central Florida. He has published over 45 articles in various academic and practitioner journals including the *Journal of Forensic Accounting, Journal of Accountancy, The CPA Journal, Internal Auditing, Journal of Business Finance and Accounting, Abacus,* and the *American Business Law Journal.* In a recent article identifying prolific authors of accounting literature, Dr. Pacini was cited as one of the three most prolific authors for Ph.D. graduates of the year 1997.

Walter J. Pagano, MPA, CPA, CFE, DABFA is a legal support services partner at Eisner LLP with over 30 years of IRS and public accounting experience in forensic accounting, fraud auditing, negotiating and settling civil and criminal tax controversies, assisting attorneys in a wide variety of white-collar crime and internal investigations, professional responsibility, accounting and tax malpractice, commercial, and civil litigation matters. Mr. Pagano has expertise in testifying in federal and state courts as well as arbitration hearings; and has served as court appointed forensic accountant. Mr. Pagano served as a revenue agent, instructor, commodity textbook author, and appeals officer with the IRS in New Jersey from 1973 to 1983. During his career in government service, Mr. Pagano assisted federal prosecutors in prosecuting tax evasion, false returns, and aiding and abetting cases.

Mark H. Taylor, Ph.D., CPA is John P. Begley Endowed Chair in Accounting at Creighton University's College of Business Administration in Omaha, Nebraska. His primary teaching and research interests are in financial statement auditing and fraud examination. Mark has previously held appointments at Brigham Young University, the University of South Carolina, and the University of Nebraska, Lincoln. Dr. Taylor earned his Ph.D. from the University of Arizona in 1994 and his research has been published in a number of leading academic journals. He serves on a number of editorial boards of research journals and fulfills consulting roles to public and private companies.

Steven C. Thompson, Ph.D., CPA is currently an Associate Professor at Texas State University, San Marcos, Texas. Dr. Thompson previously served on the faculties at Florida Gulf Coast University, the University of Houston and as an Adjunct Professor at the University of Virginia. In between his academic assignments, Steve spent two years with Ernst & Young, LLP in their Washington National Tax Education office where he re-engineered several tax education programs and developed a distance learning platform. Besides his teaching assignments, Dr. Thompson is a contributing author to many editions of various textbooks, has written numerous articles for publication in tax journals, has testified before the United States Congress on tax legislation and, for the past 4 years, has been the webmaster for the American Taxation Association. Most recently, he has joined the editorial board of the American Institute of Certified Public Accountants' *Tax Adviser Journal*. For the past 25 years, Steve has been the AICPA's lecturer on consolidated return and partnership tax issues in the summer Tax Education Program held at the University of Illinois.

INDEX

A

accountant-client communications 149, 151

accountant-client privilege 150-151, 165

admissibility, of testimony 29-30, 32-35, 37-38, 49, 52, 56-57, 121, 168

advocacy 2, 63-66, 69-70

American Institute of Certified Public Accountants (AICPA) 52, 62, 64 Code of Professional Conduct 64-65, 67, 69

Association of Certified Fraud Examiners (ACFE) 42, 73-74, 92, 97

attorney client privilege 20-22, 27, 73, 78, 149-159, 161-165

B

Barefoot v. Estelle 168

Bates stamp 4

billing records 137, 140-141

C

calculations 6, 57, 68, 122, 124

Circuit Courts
First 57
Second 57, 157-158
Fourth 54
Fifth 54
Seventh 52
Ninth 34, 51, 57

City of Tuscaloosa v. Harcros Chemicals, Inc. 36, 42

Colon v. Bic USA, Inc. 121

complaint 47, 99, 111, 130

conflict of interest 48, 65, 95

court appointed expert witness 55-56

credentials 2-3, 8, 14, 26, 31, 37, 40, 42, 73, 78, 107, 110

credibility 12, 15-16, 18, 20, 37, 40, 63, 66, 75, 78, 110, 140

criminal investigations 23, 26, 46, 53, 71-72, 150, 154, 168

cross-examination 3, 5-6, 23-24, 34, 42, 56, 58, 66, 109, 113, 116, 118, 124, 127-128, 130-133, 136, 138, 140, 145, 168

D

Daisey v. Keene Corporation 125

damages 7-9, 16, 20-21, 41-42, 72, 96, 99

Daubert on the Web 52

Daubert Tracker 52

Daubert v. Merrell Dow Pharmaceuticals, Inc. 26, 29-30, 33-38, 40-43, 45-46, 48-57, 61, 67, 111, 1 1 3 , 115-116, 118, 121, 167-169, 171, 173-174, 176-177, 179-180

demurrer 47

deposition 5, 7, 11, 14, 17, 20, 23-24, 27, 39, 59, 64-66, 73-74, 99-101, 109-111, 116-118, 130-132, 139

direct examination 24, 59, 144

discovery 8-9, 11-12, 19, 22-23, 40, 47, 58, 64, 73, 99-101, 110, 151

E

electronic communication 150, 162

evidence 3, 6, 14, 16, 20, 24-27, 30-38, 42, 48-50, 52, 58-59, 61, 67, 73-74, 82, 86, 95-96, 101, 110, 115, 127, 141, 146, 151-152, 158, 167-169, 173-179

F

fact witness 63-64, 69

Federal Bureau of Investigation (FBI) 23, 45

Federal Rules of Civil Procedure (FRCP) 23, 27, 59, 74, 151

187

Printed in the United States
40217LVS00003B/1-120